VISIONARY FAMILY MINISTRIES

FAMILY WORSHIP

Genesis

By: Rob and Amy Rienow & Jonathan and Kari Ziman

Family Worship: Genesis

By Rob and Amy Rienow / Jonathan and Kari Ziman
© 2017 Visionary Family Ministries

ISBN: 978-0-9992953-1-1

TABLE OF CONTENTS

WELCOME

When we first started having children, we had no clear plan for teaching our kids about Jesus. We just sort of assumed, "We're Christians, we go to church, how hard can it be?" Well, we made a lot of mistakes early on as we stumbled through the craziness of life as a young family. We had no clear understanding for why God had given us children, what the purpose of family was, and no intentional plan to help our children follow Jesus.

Then God showed us Deuteronomy 6:5-7:

> You shall love the LORD your God with all your heart and with all your soul and with all your might. And these words that I command you today shall be on your heart. You shall teach them diligently to your children, and shall talk of them when you sit in your house...

This is, according to Jesus, the most important commandment in the Bible. God calls us and our children to love Him with all our hearts. Immediately following this commandment, God speaks to parents, grandparents, and families. He says, "talk [about my Word] when you sit in your house." Down through the centuries this has been called "family worship"—the few moments of the day when we get together to read the Bible and pray together.

The practice of family worship has transformed our families!

Many parents are eager for their children to know and love Jesus, but lack an intentional plan to lead their children toward a life of faith. While family worship is not a magic formula that guarantees that all our children will follow Jesus for a lifetime, it is an essential ingredient of the Christian home and invites the Lord to work in the hearts of our kids.

Our hope is that this guide might be a starting point for growing faith in your family, and help you as you begin to read the Bible and pray together on a regular basis.

If we can support or encourage you in any way along this journey, please let us know!

INTRODUCTION

Start Slowly

Unfortunately, few Christian adults today grew up in homes that practiced family worship. You probably did not have this modeled for you growing up, and if you are like most Christian families today this has not been a regular part of your life. There is good news! It is never too late to begin family worship—even with teenagers or grandchildren. It is OK to start slowly. This guide is designed to give you a wide variety of creative ideas to begin family worship and spiritual conversations in your home. Don't feel pressure to use all of the ideas in each lesson. Start slowly!

Understanding The Family Worship Guide

We are excited about what kids and teens will have a chance to learn about God and His Word at church—but we believe that the spiritual teaching they receive at home is essential for their faith development. God created parents to take the lead in passing faith to their children at home, and it is the church's job to help parents be successful. That is what the family worship guide is all about. We want to give you the tools, ideas, and resources you need to impress the hearts of your children and teens with a love for God.

How To Use The Family Worship Guide

Every chapter of the worship guide has two sections: **1) Family Worship** and **2) Growing Together Throughout the Week.** If you are new to Family Worship, or it's been a while since you tried this at home, focus your time on Section 1: "Family Worship," and in particular the Bible reading and prayer. If you do nothing else, read some of the Bible and pray together. As you get more comfortable with doing this as a family you can begin to weave in the other components. Section 2: "Growing Together Throughout the Week" is provided as a series of optional ways to continue the conversation at other times during the week. Feel free to pick and choose whatever is most helpful for you! As you read through these descriptions, feel free to look ahead at the first week of ideas beginning on page 13.

The first heading for each week of the worship guide will look like this:

Following this heading you will find a suggested plan which will help you have one time of family worship that week. Each family worship time has five suggested components: 1) Activity, 2) Singing, 3) Scripture reading, 4) Talk about it, and 5) Prayer.

- Don't feel pressure to do all of these elements every time.

- If time is short, focus on the most important elements—Bible reading and prayer.

Here is a short description of the five components.

ACTIVITY

If time permits, start with something fun! These activities range from crafts, to games, to object lessons. They usually require little or no prep. Feel free to adjust and adapt the activity to fit your family. If you have teens, encourage them to lead the activity for the younger kids. If all your kids are older, you may choose to skip the activity.

SINGING

Yikes! Did you say singing? One of the ways that God invites us to worship Him is by singing. If your children are younger, and you are enthusiastic about it, they will love it, and you will lay the groundwork for singing in your family for generations to come. If your kids are all teenagers, and you have never tried singing together as a family, you may want to try this in a few months—after family worship has taken root. Younger kids will enjoy using any instruments (drums, sticks, etc). Children who have taken musical lessons can be encouraged to use their instrument and learn songs that the family likes to sing. It can be helpful to use worship CDs or DVDs. Each week we recommend some hymns and praise songs to consider. If you don't know the songs, use the internet to find the lyrics. Just type the song title into your favorite search engine.

SCRIPTURE READING

Each family worship time will be focused on a particular passage in Scripture. This is the most important part of family worship. God uses His Word to transform us!

TALK ABOUT IT

After each Scripture reading you will find a series of questions that will help your family dig into the truth of God's Word and apply it. Choose only the questions that you think will work well for your family. Change the questions as needed. The family worship guide is not a homework assignment. It is a tool for you to use, adapt, and improve to help lead your family in worshipping God at home.

PRAYER

End your family worship time with prayer. One way to pray together is to use the ACTS model. Adapt this prayer time to best suit the needs of your family.

A – Adoration, telling God how wonderful He is
C – Confession, admitting our sins to God
T – Thanksgiving, expressing our gratitude to God
S – Supplication, asking God for things we need

Growing Together Throughout the Week

After the section on family worship, you will find the section titled "Growing Together Throughout The Week." There you will find a variety of ideas for how to keep spiritual conversations going through your normal life. Use only what is helpful. Don't feel pressure to make use of all the ideas.

The first thing you will find in this section are additional questions that you can talk about with your kids during meal times, car time, etc.

FAMILY MEMORY VERSE

Each week you will find a Scripture which you may consider memorizing as a family. You may choose to write it on a 3x5 card for everyone to keep with them during the week. The more you repeat the Scripture throughout the week, the more likely you are to remember it.

CATECHISM QUESTIONS

Catechism is a fancy word for using questions and answers to teach children about God and His Word. You may be surprised how much your children love to memorize the answers to these questions. Each week, you will find a few questions and answers to learn together as a family. Kids particularly enjoy it when they can be the "catechiser"—which means they get to ask the questions of the other family members and see if they know the answer.

DIGGING DEEPER FOR TEENS

Every week you will find suggested conversations, questions, online research, or videos to watch that will help engage your teenager in a substantive conversation about God and His Word. The questions are also designed to help parents and teens deepen their relationship. When our kids are teenagers, they need us more than ever before as they are making major decisions that will impact the rest of their lives.

PRESCHOOL FUN

Here you will find fun, simple ways to help your preschooler talk with you about God and His Word.

Resources To Super-Charge Family Worship

Throughout the family worship guide we will point you to additional resources which can be a tremendous help to your family. Here are a few that we encourage you to consider in order to maximize your spiritual life at home.

The Child's Story Bible by Catherine Vos

Don't be fooled by the title. This is not a "kiddy Bible." This is the Bible in powerful story form, and it can be used as a great complement to your family Bible reading time.

Family Time Training (www.famtime.com)

When we put some creativity and fun into family worship—kids love it! That is where Family Time Training comes in. Every month they offer a free family worship activity, or you can subscribe to get full access to their entire archive!

The Big Picture Story Bible by David R. Helm

Great for preschoolers! *The Big Picture Story Bible* is designed to teach the "big story" of the Bible—connecting all the events of Scripture with Christ.

Seeds Family Worship

Fun, Scripture based songs on CD that can help your family sing together and worship God.

Genesis 1:1–2:3

God Creates the Heavens and the Earth

Activity

Words in **bold** are what you can say to lead this activity.

Supplies needed:

1. A bag of Scrabble tiles

2. If you don't have Scrabble, get a stack of 3x5 cards, or cut up paper into 50 small squares. Have each person write the letters of their name on each card or square. One card or square per letter, just like a Scrabble tile.

Let's try an experiment with this pile of alphabet letters. We need a volunteer to do the experiment first. Who wants to start? Once you have a volunteer, take all the tiles and stack them in the person's hands. **OK, in your hands are a bunch of letters. Here is what you need to do. Toss the letters into the air, and when they**

fall down they will spell your name on the floor. Ready, toss! After the letters fall to the floor, act surprised that the person's name did not appear. **I guess that didn't work. Maybe your name is too hard. Is there someone else who wants to try? I really want to make this work.** Get all the letters back into a pile, put them in the hands of the new person, and let them toss the letters again. Of course, the letters will land in a jumbled mess. Let each member of the family try the experiment.

I guess our experiment didn't work. If we want to spell our names with the tiles what do you think we need to do? We have to use our minds and intentionally put the letters together that spell our names. Ask each person to use the letters to spell out their name.

Did you know that some people think that the world came together without a plan? They think everything that we see: the planets, the clouds, the rocks, the animals, even people…just "happened." In our family worship time we are going to learn the truth about how the world was created.

Singing

Consider one or more of the following songs to praise God for His creation. Need song lyrics? Just Google the song titles.

God is Creator, by Seeds Family Worship

God of Wonders, by Third Day

At Your Name, by Phil Wickham

Scripture Reading: Genesis 1:1–2:3

Read the above Scriptures aloud as a family. Consider having different family members read different portions. In particular, consider sharing the reading of the days of creation. Remember, if your time is short, Scripture reading is the most important part of your family worship time. God uses His word to teach us and make us more like Christ.

Talk About It

Discuss the following questions as a family. The brief answers provided may help you guide the conversation as needed.

1. **If you want to bake a cake, what do you need? If you want to build a house what do you need?** In order to make things, we need the necessary ingredients or supplies.

2. **What was there before God created the universe in Genesis 1:1? What ingredients or supplies did He have to build the Universe?** Nothing! There were no rocks, plants, animals, or planets. There wasn't even any space. Even time didn't exist. There was nothing except for God Himself. God created everything out of nothing.

3. **How did God create the Universe and everything in it? What does that tell us about God?** God created all things by simply speaking them into being. Creation shows us that God is all-powerful. Imagine

how long it would take a group of people to move a mountain from one place to another. God created all the planets in the universe in an instant. Go deeper into this question by reading Romans 1:20.

4. **What part of God's creation here in Genesis 1 is the most amazing or interesting to you?**

5. **This Scripture teaches us that God created the world and everything in it. But what is God doing now? Is He just sitting back and watching everything that is happening like a watchmaker who builds a watch and then lets it run? Let's discover the answer in Colossians 1:15–16.**

Prayer

A powerful way to pray as a family is to follow the "ACTS" model. You may choose to pray through one or all of these sections. Invite anyone who wants to pray to do so.

ADORATION

In reading the Bible today, what are some of the things that we learned about God? *(He is all-powerful, He is all-knowing, He is eternal.)* **Let's begin our time in prayer by worshipping Him for who He is. We do this simply by telling God that we love Him and worship Him for these things.** A parent might want to lead this time by praying, "God we worship you today because you are all powerful. We know this because you created the whole Universe."

CONFESSION

God knows all things. He knows everything we think and everything we do. He knows the good and the bad. We also know that God loves us and invites us to confess our sins to Him. Let's confess our sins to God now. (*Initially it may be best to do this silently and personally. Although, as your family gets more comfortable praying together, it may be appropriate to confess some sins out loud. In that case, it is often valuable for a parent to be the first to pray in this section.*)

THANKSGIVING

God created everything in this amazing world. Let's take some time now and thank Him for the things He has made that we enjoy.

SUPPLICATION

God is all powerful. He can do anything! He tells us that we can come to Him with our requests. Let's use this time to ask God for the things we need, as well as asking God to help others that we know.

A parent can conclude the family worship time with a prayer of thanks to God.

Growing Together Throughout the Week

Keep the conversation about God, His Word, and His Creation going throughout the week. Consider talking about some of these questions at meal times, in the car, or before bed. Some brief answers are provided to help you guide the conversation.

1. **In Genesis 1, God says that the world He created was good. Unfortunately, we now see a lot of bad things in the world. Why do you think things like earthquakes and tornados happen?**
   When sin entered the world, it affected everything. The good world that God made became bad. Even the physical universe is broken and damaged because of sin.

2. **Why do you think God created so many different kinds of animals? Why do you think He created every person totally unique? Why do you think God made the world in color and not in black and white?**
   God loves variety, creativity, and beauty.

3. **The culture we live in says that some people are pretty, and others are not so pretty. God is the creator of each person. If we say that another person is ugly, what are we saying about God?**
   God makes each person beautiful in His eyes. Christians have to decide whether we will follow the world's standards for beauty or follow God's standards.

4. Consider getting some episodes of the Jonathan Park Radio Drama on CD. Jonathan Park is an adventure story that teaches kids about creation. Your whole family will enjoy listening and your children will learn about how the scientific evidence supports the creation account in the Bible.

Family Memory Verse

Work together as a family to memorize this verse this week.

"So God created man in his own image, in the image of God He created him; male and female He created them." (Genesis 1:27)

Catechism Questions

As you go through your week, help each other learn the answers to these important questions. You may choose to include catechism as a part of your family worship time.

1. **Who made you?** God made me

2. **What else did God make?** God made all things.

3. **Why did God make you and all things?** For his own glory.

Digging Deeper—For Teens

ONLINE

Is it reasonable to believe that God created the world? Hasn't science proved that evolution is true and that God was not needed? Gather around a computer and investigate the evidence for yourself at this website: ***www.icr.org/Evidence/***

What about the dinosaurs? Did they die in the flood or millions of years ago? Check out the latest research at ***www.answersingenesis.com.***

TALK ABOUT IT

1. If someone asked you to explain why you believe in creation and not evolution, what would you say?

2. If evolution is true and everything is here by random chance, how would that affect things like morality, meaning, purpose, and life after death?

3. Why do you think that the debate between evolution and creation is so intense? Why would those who believe in atheistic evolution be so adamant that both sides of the debate not be taught in schools, allowing students to decide for themselves? Use the websites above to help your discussion.

4. What does "resting on the seventh day" look like in your life? God worked for six days and then He rested. God tells us to do the same. Do you make Sunday a separate day for worship and rest? Find out what God says about Sabbath in Exodus 20 and Isaiah 58.

Preschool Fun

Help your preschooler increase their wonder at God's creation by going small. Get a strong magnifying glass. Go outside with your preschooler and gather some objects from nature into a paper bag. You might get a flower, pinecone, bark, pebble, or grass. Spread out the objects on a table, and take a few moments to look at each one through the magnifying glass. Talk about the things that surprise you or interest you. Let them look at their own skin. Fingerprints are cool! Talk about how amazing, smart, and powerful God is that He made all these things and more.

As mentioned in the introduction, kids of all ages love *The Child's Story Bible* by Catherine Vos. It is a great tool to go alongside your family Bible reading.

Genesis 1:26–2:25

God Creates Man and Woman

Activity

Words in **bold** are what you can say to lead this activity.

Supplies needed:

1. A piece of 8.5x11 paper for each person in the family

2. Each person will need something to draw with. Ideally, have a mix of pencils, pens, crayons, or markers.

We are going to start our family worship time with an activity. The first thing we need to do is think of three different kinds of animals. Who wants to pick the first animal? As the family comes up with three different animals, the leader should write their names down on a piece of paper. **OK, now we all need to take our piece of paper and do our best to draw a picture of each of these animals. You can use both sides of the paper if you want to.** You may need to help little ones with their drawings. Wait till everyone is done drawing their three animals. **In our Bible reading today, God gives Adam the assignment of naming all the animals. Can you imagine all the animals coming to you for you to name them? I wonder what names we would give to the animals if it was our job to name them? Let's find out. Each one of us has a picture of the three animals that we chose. If it was your job to name these animals, what would you name them? Let's think about it for a minute, and then write down the names you come up with. Do it quietly, because in a minute we will go around and get to hear the names that we all came up with.** (Give an example like, "Fluffball," if needed, to spark creativity). Wait for everyone to write down their new animal names. Help little ones as needed. Have fun going around and sharing the names that you would have given to the animals.

God created the heavens and the earth and everything in them in just six days. At the end of the sixth day, God made His most important creation—man and woman. He put them in charge of the earth and all the animals. He created marriage, and Adam and Eve were the first husband and wife. In a few minutes, we will read in the Bible about all these things.

Singing

Consider one or more of the following songs to praise God for His creation.

The Word of the Lord, by Seeds Family Worship

This is My Father's World, by Fernando Ortega

Glorious Day, by Kristian Stanfill

Scripture Reading: Genesis 1:26–2:25

Read the above Scripture aloud as a family. Consider having different family members read different portions of the passage.

Talk About It

Discuss the following questions as a family. Feel free to skip questions, or add new ones as appropriate. The brief answers may help you guide the conversation as needed.

1. **What is the first thing that God tells Adam and Eve he wants them to do?** In Genesis 1:28 God says, "Be fruitful and multiply and fill the earth and subdue it." God wants the earth filled with people who love Him and worship Him.

2. **In Genesis 1:29, what does God tell Adam and Eve that they are allowed to eat?** Only veggies! Why do you think that Christians now believe it is OK to eat meat? For the answer take a look at Genesis 9:1–3.

3. **Can you use a map to find where the Garden of Eden was?** There are four rivers named in Genesis 2:10–14. We still know where two of those rivers are—the Tigris and Euphrates. Get a map or go online to see if you can find the part of the world where the Garden of Eden was situated.

4. **In Genesis 2:18 God says that it is not good for the man to be alone. What is God's solution to Adam being alone?** God creates Eve who becomes Adam's wife. God doesn't want us to be alone. This is why God has given us our family at home, and our spiritual family at church.

5. **What was the most interesting thing for you in the Scripture that we looked at today? What would you like to learn more about?**

Prayer

A powerful way to pray as a family is to follow the "ACTS" model. You may choose to pray through one or all of these sections. Invite anyone who wants to pray to do so.

ADORATION

In reading the Bible today, what are some of the things that we learned about God? *(He created the world and all of life in 6 days. He created man and woman with equal value, and humans are totally different from the animals. He created marriage and family as a special gift.)* Begin your prayer time by telling God that you love Him and worship Him for these things.

CONFESSION

God knows all things. He knows everything we think and everything we do. He knows the good and the bad. We also know that God loves us and invites us to confess our sins to Him. Let's confess our sins to God now. *(It is valuable for a parent to be the first to pray in this section.)*

THANKSGIVING

Creation is filled with things to be thankful for. Take time now and thank God for the things He created that you enjoy. The Scripture today told us of God's creation of the first family. Give thanks for your family and extended family.

SUPPLICATION

God created the entire Universe in six days. His power knows no limitations. Amazingly, God says that we can pray to Him and bring our requests to Him.

Let's use this time to ask God for the things we need, as well as asking God to help others that we know.

A parent can conclude the family worship time with a prayer of thanks to God.

Growing Together Throughout the Week

Keep the conversation about God, His Word, and His Creation going throughout the week. Consider talking about some of these questions at meal times, in the car, or before bed. Some brief answers are provided to help you guide the conversation.

1. **In Genesis 2:15–17, God tells us about a special instruction that He gave to Adam and Eve. He told them that they could eat from any tree in the garden, except for one. What does this tell us about God?**
   God created man and woman with tremendous freedom. Some people see God as someone who doesn't ever want us to be happy. If that was the case, He would have told Adam and Eve that all the trees were off limits. God gives His people wonderful freedom to make choices, and the choices we make are very important to Him.

2. **In Genesis 2:15 God gives Adam a job. What was it?**
   To take care of the garden. God created work as something we can do to please Him and glorify Him. Is this the way we think about the work we have to do? Often, we think of work as something bad. How can your family help each other do your work to please God and glorify Him?

3. **What does God do in Genesis 2:2?**
   He rests on the seventh day and calls it holy. How should our family make Sunday a day of rest and a holy day? Talk about this as a family and pray together about ways that you can make Sunday a holy day of rest.

Family Memory Verse

Work together as a family to memorize this verse this week.

"And God blessed them. And God said to them, 'Be fruitful and multiply and fill the earth and subdue it.'" (Genesis 1:28)

Catechism Questions

As you go through your week, help each other learn the answers to these important questions. You may choose to include catechism as a part of your family worship time.

Learn more about how to use catechism questions in the Introduction.

4. **How can you glorify God?** By loving Him and doing what He commands

5. **Why should you glorify God?** Because He made me and takes care of me.

Digging Deeper—For Teens

ONLINE

Do you know where the Garden of Eden was situated? There are a number of theories. Use the clues in Genesis 2:10–14 and review the research at **www.icr.org**.

TALK ABOUT IT

1. In Genesis 1:27, God says that He created both man and woman in His image. This was a shocking teaching in the ancient world, which believed that men were more important than women. Jesus also treated women and men with equal value and dignity. What are the implications of this Biblical teaching for our culture today? *For more on how Christianity has protected and given dignity to women read the book "What if Jesus Had Never Been Born?" by D. James Kennedy.*

2. In Genesis 1:28, God blesses Adam and Eve and calls them to fill the earth by having children, and to rule over the earth and the animals. Humans are not considered "animals" by God. If God put people in charge of the earth, what does that mean for how we care for the earth? In what ways do some people today treat animals as more important than people?

3. In Genesis 2:24, we learn that marriage is to be between one man and one woman. What would you say if a friend asked you, "Why isn't it OK for two people of the same sex to get married?"

4. In Genesis 2:25, we learn that God created sexuality as something good and blessed. Sexuality is a gift that God created to be used only in monogamous (one-on-one), heterosexual (one man, one woman), marriage (covenant relationship). In what ways has the world twisted this gift of sexuality?

Preschool Fun

Get a mirror or bring the kids into a room that has a mirror. Let each one of them put their face up close to the mirror and look at their features. Talk about the color of your eyes, the shape of your nose, and any other features you want to talk about. Let the kids look at your reflection. In what ways do we look the same? In what ways do we look different? Use this opportunity to teach the children that God made each one of us unique—there is no one else in the world like them. Read Genesis 1:27–28 out loud and talk about how God made us to reflect His image to others.

Genesis 3:1–24

Adam and Eve Sin Against God

Activity

Words in **bold** are what you can say to lead this activity. Remember, if you are short on time, just focus on the Scripture reading and prayer.

Supplies needed: None

We are going to start tonight with one of the oldest and best games there is. We are going to play hide and seek. If you have little children, they will be ready to go! If you have a mix of elementary and junior high/high school age kids, talk with the older kids before starting the activity and ask them to be the ones who lead the game for the family. **The first thing we need to do is choose someone who will be "it." Who wants to volunteer?** Once you have your volunteer, have them count slowly to 30, and let the game begin! The last one to be found wins.

Mix up the game however you want to. Play inside, outside, or both. You can also play "sardines" where instead of everyone hiding and one person going to find them, one person hides and it is the job of everyone else to try and find the one person hiding. When a person finds the one "hider" they should quietly join them in their hiding place. It may get a little tight! If someone else finds the two "hiders" they also join them. The last person left searching gets to be the one to hide the next round. After you play a couple of rounds, gather the family back together.

That was fun! The reason we just played that game is because it helps us to think about what we are going to find in our Bible reading today. Last week we read Genesis chapter 2 and we learned how God made Adam and Eve special and separate from all the animals. He gave them a beautiful garden and a beautiful marriage. They only had one rule. They must not eat from one tree in the garden; the tree of the knowledge of good and evil. Did they obey God or disobey God? Allow kids to answer. That is right, they disobeyed, and do you know what they did after that? They hid from God.

Singing

Consider one or more of the following songs to worship God for His holiness.

Mighty to Save, by Seeds Family Worship

Wonderful Merciful Savior

My Victory, by David Crowder

Scripture Reading: Genesis 3:1–24

Read the above Scripture aloud as a family. Consider having different family members read different portions of the passage.

Talk About It

Discuss the following questions as a family. Feel free to skip questions, or add new ones as appropriate. The brief answers may help you guide the conversation as needed.

1. **In Genesis 3:1 we learn that Satan came to Eve in the form of a snake. What did Satan first say to Eve to tempt her?** Satan said, "Did God really say, 'You shall not eat of any tree in the garden?'"

2. **The first four words of Satan's temptation are perhaps the most important, "Did God actually say?" Why do you think Satan began his temptation with these words?** Satan's first objective is for us to doubt God and His Word. If Satan can lead us to not believe what God has said in the Bible, then we are vulnerable to every lie and every temptation.

3. **According to Genesis 3:6, where was Adam when Eve was being tempted?** He was standing there with her.

4. **Why do you think that Adam and Eve hid from God after they had sinned against Him?** They were ashamed of their sin. We often act

like Adam and Eve when we try and cover up and lie about the wrong things we have done. Learning to confess our sins in our family is one of the most important things we can do.

5. **What were the consequences for Eve and all future women because of her sin? What were the consequences for Adam and all future men because of his sin?** Look for the answers in Genesis 3:16–19.

6. **In Genesis 3:15 we find the first promise about Jesus. What is it?** God curses Satan and promises that one day the offspring of a woman would crush Satan's head, but Satan would strike his heel. Even though Satan would hurt Jesus at the cross, Jesus crushed Satan through His resurrection.

Prayer

A powerful way to pray as a family is to follow the "ACTS" model. You may choose to pray through one or all of these sections. Invite anyone who wants to pray to do so.

ADORATION

In reading the Bible today, what are some of the things that we learned about God? *(He is holy and perfect. He is loving because He did not destroy Adam and Eve but rather made coverings for them, promised them a Savior, and enabled them to* *continue to fulfill God's plan to fill the earth with His people.)* Praise God for these things.

CONFESSION

Genesis 3 is a serious chapter about sin. Adam and Eve hid from God instead of confessing. Even after they were caught Adam blamed Eve and God, and Eve blamed the serpent. We need to take responsibility for our own sin. Let's confess our sins to God now. *(It is valuable for a parent to be the first to pray in this section.)*

THANKSGIVING

Let's take some time now to thank God for His forgiveness. Thank Him that He does not treat us as our sins deserve, but that He is a God of second chances.

SUPPLICATION

Take time to present your requests to God. A parent can conclude this time with a brief prayer of thanks to God.

Growing Together Throughout the Week

Keep the conversation going about God and His word throughout the week. Consider talking about some of these questions at meal times, in the car, or before bed.

1. **What did Adam say to God when God asked him if he had eaten from the tree of the knowledge of good and evil? (Genesis 3:12)**
   Adam first blamed Eve. The first words out of his mouth were, "The woman..." Adam then blamed God, "The woman whome you gave to be with me..." Finally, after blaming both Eve and God, Adam said, "I ate [the fruit]." Why do you think it is so hard for us to admit when we do things wrong?

2. **In Genesis 2:17 God promises that if Adam and Eve eat the fruit of the tree, they will surely die. They did eat the fruit, so why didn't they die?**
   When God promised that they would surely die, this meant two things. First, it meant that they would die spiritually. This happened immediately after their sin. Instead of having a perfect holy nature, they now had a wicked sinful nature. Second, before Adam and Eve sinned they had bodies that would never die. Because of their sin, immediately their bodies began to move toward certain death.

3. **Satan wanted Eve to believe that God was a liar. In reality, Satan was the liar and Eve chose to believe Satan rather than God. Can you think of ways that Satan tries to get us to believe his lies today? Can you think of ways that Satan tries to convince us that the Bible is not true?**
   Talk about ways that your family can help each other fight against Satan's lies and believe the Bible.

Family Memory Verse

Work together as a family to memorize this verse this week.

"All Scripture is breathed out by God and profitable for teaching, for reproof, for correction, and for training in righteousness." (2 Timothy 3:16)

Catechism Questions

As you go through your week, help each other learn the answers to these important questions. You may choose to include catechism as a part of your family worship time.

6. **Are there more gods than one?** No, there is only one God.

7. **In how many persons does this one God exist?** In three persons.

8. **Who are they?** The Father, the Son, and the Holy Spirit.

Digging Deeper—For Teens

1. If Eve was the one who ate the fruit, why did God confront Adam? (Genesis 3:11–12) *God created Adam to be the leader in the marriage relationship. God had commanded Adam not to eat of the tree to before Eve was created. Adam was the spiritual head of the human race. Read more about this in Romans 5:12-19.*

2. What does it mean in Genesis 3:17 when God says, "cursed is the ground" and then later God tells Adam, "by the sweat of your face you shall eat bread." *Before sin entered the world, work was a joy. Now, because sin infected everything, even the plants and animals, man's work would be painfully difficult.*

3. In Genesis 3 we see Adam and Eve succumbing quickly to temptation. As a result, all of their children (including you and me) have a sinful nature. In what ways can we battle temptation today? What are the most difficult temptations you face? How did Jesus battle temptation? *Find out in Luke 4.*

4. After Adam and Eve sinned, they were ashamed that they were naked. Sin warped even their sexuality. God originally created sex for three reasons: uniting the spirits of husband and wife, creating children, and pleasure. How has Satan twisted God's purposes for sex in our culture today? *One of Satan's top priorities in this area is to keep parents and teens from talking openly about sex, pornography, and sexual*

temptation. What would it take to build open communication in your home about these important issues?

Preschool Fun

Get a cereal bowl and fill it with water. Give your preschooler the chance to put a drop of food coloring in the water. Stir it together. Consider doing this with a few different bowls and with different colors. Ask your preschooler if there is any way to take the color out of the water. No. Once the water is stained it can't be easily cleaned again. In a similar way, once Adam and Eve sinned, they were stained with sin. They could not get themselves clean again. Only God could make a way for them to be cleaned and forgiven.

Genesis 4:1–16

Cain Rebels Against God

Activity

Words in **bold** are what you can say to lead this activity. If time is short, focus on the Bible reading and prayer sections.

Supplies needed:

1. A glass jar which has an opening just large enough for a child to slip their hand in and out.

2. A small ball that just fits through the opening of the jar.

I have a challenge for you. In this jar I have a treasure! Yes, I know it looks like a ball. But it is a very valuable ball. Who would like to try to reach in and get the ball? Be sure to grab it tightly. Wrap your whole hand around it and pull it out. It is against the rules to tip the jar over.

If the jar is the right size the child will be able to slip his or her hand through the opening, but when they make a fist around the ball, they will not be able to get their hand out. Give each child a chance to try the game.

What happened? You were able to put your hand into the jar, but when you made a fist around the ball, you were not able to take your hand out. Imagine if you never let go of the ball! You never would have been able to get out.

I wanted to show you this because it is a picture of how we can get trapped in sin. When we sin, God wants us to confess, let go of the sin, and return to Him. If we hold on to the sin, we can't get free. In a minute, when we read the Bible together, we are going to see an example of how this happened to someone.

Singing

Consider one or more of the following songs to offer your hearts to the Lord in worship. Feel free to choose your own songs from YouTube, or use a worship CD or DVD. Consider getting the CD "Shout The Word: Trust In the Lord." Or any of the CD's from Seeds Family Worship.

Undivided Heart, by Seeds Family Worship

Before the Throne of God Above, by Shane and Shane

O Come to the Altar

Scripture Reading: Genesis 4:1–16

Read the above Scripture aloud as a family. Consider having different family members read different portions of the passage.

If you have multiple times of family worship this week, consider reading the rest of chapter 4, as well as Hebrews 11:1–4 where we learn more about Cain and Abel.

Talk About It

Discuss the following questions as a family. Feel free to skip questions, or add new ones as appropriate. The brief answers in italics may help you guide the conversation as needed.

1. **What sacrifice did Cain bring to God?** He brought "some of the fruits of the soil" which most likely means fruits, vegetables, or grains. What did Abel bring? Abel brought the best meat from his best sheep.

2. **Read Hebrews 11:4. Why do you think that God accepted Abel's sacrifice but not Cain's?** It may be that Abel gave the best, while Cain did not. The best explanation is found in Hebrews 11:4 where we learn that Abel gave his sacrifice in faith (believing God with a humble heart) while Cain apparently did not.

3. **When God accepted Abel's offering but not Cain's, how did Cain respond?** He became very angry.

4. **Anger can be a very dangerous thing in a family. How does our family handle our anger?** You may need to encourage the family to be honest about how they feel about how anger is handled in the family. Parents can set a great example here by confessing any problems we have with anger (raising our voice, being harsh, etc).

5. **God gave Cain a chance to repent and "do what is right." But Cain, in his anger, did not let go of his sin. What happened because Cain did not let go of his sin?** His sin multiplied, leading to murder.

6. **When God confronted Cain about where Abel was, Cain asked God, "Am I my brother's keeper?" What is the answer to that question?** The answer is "yes" Cain was his brother's keeper. Siblings are responsible before God to protect each other and stick together.

7. **How can the siblings in your family increase their commitment to care for and protect each other?**

8. **In Genesis 3, God did not destroy Adam and Eve when they sinned, but gave them a second chance. Here God does the same with Cain. What does that tell us about God?** God is loving, forgiving, fair, and just. He always takes sin seriously, and He continues to love those who have trusted in Jesus as their Savior.

Prayer

A powerful way to pray as a family is to follow the "ACTS" model. You may choose to pray through one or all of these sections. Invite anyone who wants to pray to do so.

ADORATION

In reading the Bible today, what are some of the things that we learned about God? *He is compassionate (His heart was broken over Abel's death). He is fair (He dealt with Cain's sin). He is gracious (He protected Cain).* Begin your prayer time by telling God that you love Him and worship Him for these things.

CONFESSION

Genesis 4 focuses our attention on sin between brothers. If God has blessed you with siblings, take time now to confess any sins that you may have committed against them. *It is valuable for a parent to be the first to pray in this section.*

THANKSGIVING

Let's take some time now to thank God for His blessings. Thank Him for the roof over your head, for the food you enjoyed today. Thank him for your siblings (if you have siblings), and more broadly for your your brothers and sisters in Christ at church.

SUPPLICATION

Take time to present your requests to God. Specifically ask God to transform and heal any hurting sibling relationships in your family.

Growing Together Throughout the Week

Consider talking about some of these questions at meal times, in the car, or before bed. Some brief answers are provided to help you guide the conversation.

1. **God warned Cain that because of his angry response and lack of faith, "sin was crouching at [his] door." What do you think God meant by this warning?**

   When we choose to sin, or give in to anger, the power of that sin increases in our hearts. Satan doesn't just want us to play with sin, He wants sin to own us and control us. For instance, people who tell little lies turn into people who tell big lies. People who steal a little turn into people who steal a lot.

2. **After Cain brought the sacrifice that God rejected, God gave Cain a chance to try again. God encouraged him, "If you do what is right, will you not be accepted?" Cain did not accept this second chance**

from God. **Why do you think Cain did not tell God that he was sorry and seek to give God his best the next time?**

Cain gave into his anger. He had a wonderful chance to repent and turn to God. This is an important lesson for us in our families. When we do things that are wrong, when we hurt each other, it is so important that we apologize quickly, seek forgiveness, and try to do better the next time.

3. **God did not let Cain get away with his sin. Sometimes it seems like people are able to do all sorts of terrible things and they "get away with it." Do you think it is possible to do something wrong and get away with it?**

God always deals with all sin. No one will "get away" with anything. This means that 1) We can trust God that He will deal with all evil in His perfect time, and 2) We must take all of our sin seriously and put our full faith and trust in Jesus for the forgiveness of our sins. We can praise God that Jesus took the punishment for all our sins on the cross so that we might be forgiven.

Family Memory Verse

Work together as a family to memorize this verse this week.

"And if you do not do well, sin is crouching at the door. Its desire is contrary to you, but you must rule over it." (Genesis 4:7b)

Catechism Questions

If you have not tried using the catechism questions yet, this is a great week to start. Go back to page 19 and start with those questions.

On the other hand, if you have been working on the catechism questions from the first three weeks, use this week to review what you have already been working on.

Digging Deeper—For Teens

Questions for parents and teens to discuss together:

1. Where did Cain get his wife? Search for the answer by searching for "Cain's wife" at the website **www.answersingenesis.com.**

2. Is it possible to be angry and not sin? Can you think of any situations where it is appropriate to be angry? Take a look at the following Scriptures to explore this question further. Ephesians 4:26, Mark 10:13–15, Colossians 3:8, James 1:20.

3. In Genesis 3, Adam blamed Eve and God for his sin. Eve blamed the serpent. Here in Genesis 4, Cain does not want to be responsible for Abel. Why do you think it is so hard for us to take responsibility and admit when we sin?

4. Are you the oldest child in the family? If so, what roles and responsibilities does God want you to play for those younger than you? What steps could you take to grow as the oldest sibling in the family?

Preschool Fun

Take five minutes and play charades with your preschooler. The parent can go first by acting something out (choose something simple) and see if your child can guess what it is. Encourage them to try. They may need a little help. After playing a couple of rounds take a moment and explain how God wants to show His love through us every day. Other people see Jesus in us when we are kind, respectful, helpful, and obedient.

AN ENCOURAGEMENT FOR PARENTS

Why do you think it is so hard to take time for family worship? Or when you do try, why is it often so difficult and frustrating?

Family worship is a challenge because Satan doesn't want you to do it! He will throw everything he can at your family to stop you. Why does he care so much? Because family worship is the spiritual engine that powers your home, builds your relationships, and helps pass faith to your children. So be encouraged! Pray for God to give you strength, energy, patience, grace and enthusiasm. And don't give up—even one brief moment of Bible reading and prayer this week can make a huge difference!

Genesis 6:1–7:24

God Floods the Earth

Activity

Words in **bold** are what you can say to lead this activity.

(Optional supplies: A large spool of fishing line or string)

Have you ever wondered exactly how big Noah's ark was? If two of every kind of animal could fit on the ark, it must have been huge...but how huge? The Bible tells us the dimensions of the ark. Let's take a look and see what it says. Would someone be willing to read Genesis 6:15? Your Bible translation may list the dimensions in feet or cubits. The activity is more fun if you talk about the ancient measurement of cubits. **OK, so the ark was 300 cubits long, 50 cubits wide, and 30 cubits high. But what is a cubit? A cubit was about 18", or one and a half 12" rulers. It is about the distance from your elbow to the ends of your fingers. Let's all hold up our arms and look at how long a cubit is. Now we need to figure out how long 300 cubits would be.** Find the "longest" place in your house. It might be a hallway, or where two rooms connect. If weather is nice, this is even more fun outside. **Let's see how many cubits we can put together. Use your arms to**

start on one end of the room/hall and measure out one cubit at a time. How many cubits long is this room/hall? If you are doing this outside, see if the kids can measure out 100 cubits using their arm as a ruler. If you do it inside, your room/hall will likely measure somewhere between 10 and 40 cubits. You can run fishing line or string across the span that you measured. Then figure out how much bigger the ark would have been compared to your area. For instance, if you measured 15 cubits, then the ark would be 20 times longer than that!

Here is another way we might think about how big the ark was. Think of a football field. A football field is 300 feet long. The ark was 450 feet long! Do you know how high our house is? You can estimate about 12 feet per floor of your house. **The ark was 30 cubits high—that is 45 feet! So imagine a house three stories high, 75 feet wide, and one and a half football fields long!**

During our family worship time we are going to read the true story of Noah's ark and the terrible flood.

Singing

Consider one or more of the following songs to praise God for His creation. Use the resources in the introduction to find music and lyrics for suggested songs.

The Rock Eternal, by Seeds Family Worship

Awesome God, by Rich Mullins

Holy, Holy, Holy

Scripture Reading: Genesis 6:1–7:24

Read the above Scriptures aloud as a family. This is a longer section, so consider having different family members read different portions:

Talk About It

Discuss the following questions as a family. The brief answers provided may help you guide the conversation as needed.

1. **The flood is one of the most well known events in the Bible and in history. It is also a very sad story. The earth had become a terrible place because of sin. According to Genesis 6:5 how bad was it?** This was the most terrible time in the history of the world. There will never be another time like this. God says in this verse that everything people were thinking and doing was "only evil all the time."

2. **In Genesis 6:6 it says that God's heart was filled with pain. What does that tell us about God?** God loves us. He did not create us for sin, but created us to know Him and love Him. The world was filled with violence and injustice—and everyone was guilty. God's heart was filled with pain because of His love for us.

3. **What did God decide to do? (Look at Genesis 6:7)** God is holy and he brings judgment against sin. He chose to destroy the earth with a flood, but to save a righteous family—Noah and his wife, their three sons, and their wives.

4. **Did God flood the whole earth or just a part of it?** Let's look at Genesis 6:17, 7:4, and 7:19 for clues.

5. **In Genesis 7:7–10 we find out an important order for how things happened. Let's read those verses together. What happened, and why is it important?** After the ark was built (it likely took 100 years to build), Noah and his family entered the ark. After they got on, God brought all the animals to the ark and they entered. Then seven days later the flood began. Noah had to have faith in God. He built the ark and entered it before the animals came, and before the rain started.

6. **Noah had incredible faith. When God told him to build an ark on dry land, he obeyed. How can we learn from Noah's obedience to God?** God has given us His Word which tells us how He wants us to live each day. Every day we have a choice of whether we will live like the world, or obey God.

Prayer

A powerful way to pray as a family is to follow the "ACTS" model. You may choose to pray through one or all of these sections. Invite anyone who wants to pray to do so.

ADORATION

In reading the Bible today, what are some of the things that we learned about God? *(He is holy and just. His heart breaks when we sin, and He also brings judgment against sin.)* **Let's begin our time in prayer by worshipping him for who He is—for His love and His holiness.**

CONFESSION

We read a very serious and sad passage from the Bible. Sin is very serious to God. Thankfully, just as God made a way for Noah to be saved, God has made a way for us to be saved through Jesus. Everyone in this family sins every day. But because of Jesus we can confess our sins and experience forgiveness. Let's confess our sins to God now. *It is important that a parent begin this time of confession. Kids need to see parents set the example of how to humbly admit and confess sin.*

THANKSGIVING

Thank God for saving Noah and his family—and for filling the earth once again with beauty.

SUPPLICATION

God showed his tremendous power in the flood. The Bible says that we can pray and ask God for his help with things we are concerned and anxious about. Let's ask God for the things we need.

A parent can conclude the family worship time with a prayer of thanks to God.

Growing Together Throughout the Week

Keep the conversation about God, His Word, and His Creation going throughout the week. Consider talking about some of these questions at meal times, in the car, or before bed. Some brief answers are provided to help you guide the conversation.

1. **How do you think you would have felt if you were Noah, spending 120 years building the ark on dry ground?**
   He may have had many doubts and had people making fun of him. Talk about times when obeying God is hard.

2. **God did not just save Noah, but his whole family. Noah's family worked together to build the ark and from this family has come every person alive today. How might God be calling our family to work together to honor God?**

3. **There was only one way to escape the waters of the flood—and that was to be on the ark. In the same way there is only one way to escape God's judgment of our sin, and that is to believe in Jesus Christ. Ask your child if they have made the decision to trust in Christ alone for the forgiveness of their sins.**
   If your child has already made this decision, this is a good opportunity for them to verbally affirm it to you. If they have not chosen to trust Christ, it will be an opportunity for them to do so.

4. **Go to your computer and use an image search to find pictures/ illustrations of Noah's Ark. Based on the dimensions of the ark given in Genesis 6, which of the pictures are the most accurate? Which are the least accurate?**

5. **How do you think Noah's sons felt helping their father succeed with the mission God had given him?**
   Talk as a family about ways that parents, kids, and siblings in your home can work together to honor God, serve your church, and make a difference in your community.

Family Memory Verse

Work together as a family to memorize this verse this week.

"Noah did this; he did all that God commanded him." (Genesis 6:22)

Catechism Questions

As you go through your week, help each other learn the answers to these important questions. You may choose to include catechism as a part of your family worship time.

9. **What is God?** God is a Spirit, and does not have a body like men.

10. **Where is God?** God is everywhere.

11. **Can you see God?** No, I cannot see God, but He always sees me.

Digging Deeper—For Teens

1. Noah was saved from the flood because of God's grace, and because Noah believed God. What similarities are there to how we are saved from our sins?

2. The Bible tells us about this global flood. But did you know that there are over 200 other flood stories from cultures all around the world? How could people groups from all over the world have developed

similar "legends" about a global flood? For more on this research visit **www.icr.org** and search for "tradition global flood." Scroll down to the "article" section.

3. God is full of love and full of justice. How has God been patient with you? How has God disciplined you?

4. Noah and his family entered the ark through "one door." Do you believe there is symbolism there for how we are saved today? Read John 14:6.

5. Are you into science? Do you think that the ark could really hold all those animals? Find out what the research says. Go to **www.christiananwers.net** and search for *'could Noah's ark really hold all the animals'*

Preschool Fun

Find a big cardboard box. A large laundry basket will work too. Help your preschooler decorate the box to look like Noah's ark. Encourage siblings to help out. Once the ark is ready, try to arrange as many stuffed animals as possible—two by two. Line them up in front of the ark. When you are ready, your preschooler can jump in "the ark" and the animals can be piled on. Feel free to experience some imaginary storms while the flood waters rise. Have your camera ready. There may be a good picture here!

Genesis 8:1–9:17

God Saves Noah

Activity

Words in **bold** are what you can say to lead this activity.

Supplies needed:

1. Glass of water

2. Masking tape

3. Flashlight

4. a CD or DVD

When was the last time you saw a rainbow? Do you remember where you were? Give people a chance to share. **Can anyone name all the colors in the rainbow?** Red, Orange, Yellow, Green, Blue, Indigo, and Violet (ROY-G-BIV). **To begin our family worship time, I want to see if we can make our own rainbows. Do you**

think that is possible? What do you think we could use from around the house to make a rainbow? See what ideas the family comes up with. Below are two ideas you can use. Good luck!

Idea #1: Get a glass and fill it with water. Put the glass of water on the edge of a counter. On the floor below the counter put a white piece of paper. Use the masking tape and put a piece of tape across the top and bottom of the flashlight. When you are done, rather than a circle of light, there will be a horizontal band of light—like a movie screen. Turn out the lights and shine the flashlight down through the water onto the paper on the floor. The flashlight should be above the glass of water, shining down through the water at an angle. With just the right angle, a small rainbow will appear on the paper.

Idea #2: Find a CD or DVD. Dim the lights and use the flashlight to create a rainbow on the back of the disc. Let each person in the family give it a try. See if you can get the disc to reflect a rainbow onto a white piece of paper. For a more dramatic affect during the daytime, use the CD or DVD to create a reflection of the sunlight onto a white piece of paper. It may help to tape the white paper onto a sheet of black paper to increase the reflection.

We did a great job making a little rainbow. God made light, and all those colors are "inside" the light that we see. We can make little rainbows on pieces of paper, but only God can make rainbows that stretch from one end of the horizon to the other. God created the rainbow for a very special purpose. Every time we see a rainbow God wants us to remember something important. In our family worship time we are going to discover what that is.

Singing

Consider one or more of the following songs to praise God for His creation. Use the resources in the introduction to find music and lyrics for suggested songs.

Do Not Fear, by Seeds Family Worship

Oceans, by Hillsong

Your Love is Deep, by Jaime Smith

Scripture Reading: Genesis 8:1–9:17

Read the above Scriptures aloud as a family. This is a longer section, so consider having different family members read different portions.

Talk About It

Discuss the following questions as a family. The brief answers provided may help you guide the conversation as needed.

1. **At the end of Genesis 7 we read that the entire earth was flooded, but Noah and his family were alive in the ark. The first verse of chapter 8 is the center of the story. What does Genesis 8:1 say and why is it important?** "But God remembered Noah." The story of the

flood is about both judgment and salvation. Imagine how Noah and his family must have felt, seemingly all alone, floating above the world. But they were not alone—God remembered them.

2. **When the dove came back with the olive leaf, what did that tell Noah?** Noah knew that the water had gone down enough so that olive trees had started to grow and produce new leaves again. It was almost time to get off the ark! When the dove did not return seven days later, that was the sign that the time had come.

3. **What was the first thing that Noah did after he got off the ark?** Noah built an altar and gave thanks to God (Genesis 8:20).

4. **God rescued Noah, and Noah immediately thanked God. As a family, how well do we thank God when He takes care of us?** Have a discussion about how easy it is to pray for God's help and provision, but then forget to thank Him when He answers those prayers. Talk together as a family about how you can help each other thank God right away when His blessings come.

5. **A few minutes ago we talked about how when Noah was floating above the world, God remembered him. Have you ever felt like God forgot about you? Have you ever felt like He was very far away from you?** This is a good opportunity for parents to take the lead and talk about what it means to have faith, and struggle with having faith, during hard times.

6. **Look at Genesis 9:12–16. There we find a promise that God made to Noah, a promise that He has kept every day since then. What was the promise and how do we know He made the promise?** God promised to never again flood the whole earth. God said that the rainbow would be the sign of His promise. When your family sees a rainbow, that is a great time to remind each other about God's judgment against sin, God's salvation of Noah and his family, and God's promise to never again flood the whole earth.

Prayer

A powerful way to pray as a family is to follow the "ACTS" model. You may choose to pray through one or all of these sections. Invite anyone who wants to pray to do so.

ADORATION

In reading the Bible today, what are some of the things that we learned about God? (*He is loving. He remembers us. He keeps His promises*). **Let's begin our prayer time by worshipping God for these things.**

CONFESSION

Our Bible passage today tells us that Noah was a righteous man. This does not mean that he never did anything wrong. But righteous people admit it when they sin. They confess their sins to God. God loves us so much! He tells us that

when we confess our sins, we can be forgiven. *It is important that a parent begin this time of confession. Kids need to see parents set the example of how to humbly admit and confess sin.*

THANKSGIVING

Can you imagine how thankful Noah and his family were when they put their feet on the dry ground again? They immediately gave thanks to God. Consider the many ways God has blessed your family. Thank Him for those things now.

SUPPLICATION

God showed His tremendous power in the flood. The Bible says that we can pray and ask God for His help with things we are concerned and anxious about. Let's ask God for the things we need.

A parent can conclude the family worship time with a prayer of thanks to God.

Growing Together Throughout the Week

Keep the conversation about God and His Word going throughout the week. Consider talking about some of these questions at meal times, in the car, or before bed. Some brief answers are provided to help you guide the conversation.

1. **The Bible says that Noah lived for 950 years! (Genesis 9:28–29) Consult some resources at *www.icr.org* to learn how this might be possible.**
   For example, people lived much longer in those days. Some believe this is because sicknesses and diseases came into the world with sin. Before sin, the world was perfect, without sickness and death. As the world became more sinful, sicknesses and diseases also became more severe, so humans began to have shorter and shorter lifespans

2. **When God created Adam and Eve, He gave them only fruits and vegetables to eat. But Christians today are allowed to eat meat. Why? (Genesis 9:2–3).**
   After the flood, God gave us both animals and plants to eat.

3. **Do you think that people are born "basically good" or "basically bad?" (Genesis 8:21). What does this tell us about God's love for us?**
   This is one of the many passages that teaches the doctrine of "original sin"—that we are born sinful, not good. We are "wired up" to do

wrong, not right. Despite this, God loves us, and has made a plan for us to be redeemed. Can we see any evidence of original sin in the behavior of small children?

4. **How long was Noah and his family on the ark? You can figure it out. Get a pencil and paper. Use the clues from Genesis 7:4–8:19.**

5. **How do you think Noah's sons felt helping their father succeed with the mission God had given him?**
   Talk as a family about ways that parents, kids, and siblings in your home can work together to honor God, serve your church, and make a difference in your community.

Family Memory Verse

Work together as a family to memorize this verse this week.

"I establish my covenant with you, that never again shall all flesh be cut off by the waters of the flood, and never again shall there be a flood to destroy the earth." (Genesis 9:11)

Catechism Questions

As you go through your week, help each other learn the answers to these important questions. You may choose to include catechism as a part of your family worship time.

12. Does God know all things? Yes; nothing can be hidden from God.

13. Can God do all things? Yes; God can do anything He wants.

14. Where do you learn to love and obey God? In the Bible alone.

Digging Deeper—For Teens

1. After God made Adam and Eve, He told them to be fruitful, multiply, and fill the earth. After Noah and his family exited the ark, God said the same thing to them. In fact, God says it twice in Genesis 9. From the very beginning, God has said that He wants the earth filled with people who love Him. But some suggest that the earth is overpopulated and that it is bad for the planet for humans to "be fruitful and multiply." What do you think?

2. Dig deeper. Is the earth really overpopulated? This will take some work but it will be worth it. Get out a calculator. Use the internet to get the current population of the earth. Write that number down. Now let's consider a space the size of the state of Texas. Texas is about 268,500 square miles. Every square mile has 27,878,400 square feet in it. You can multiply those two numbers to get the total number of square feet in Texas. Almost done. Take your gigantic square footage of Texas number, and divide it by the population of the earth.

3. Here is what your final number means. If you were to take the entire population of the earth, and put everyone in Texas, that is how many

square feet they would have—all to themselves. Does this surprise you? Do you think that God still wants His people to *"be fruitful and multiply, increase greatly on the earth and multiply in it"* (Genesis 9:7)?

4. When they got off the ark, Noah was quick to thank God for saving him and his family. He built an altar to worship God. Why do you think it is so easy for us to take God's blessings for granted and not give Him the thanks and praise He deserves? How could you become a more thankful person?

Preschool Fun

Help your preschooler make a rainbow. You can use crayons, markers, construction paper—anything that you will enjoy doing together. Talk with your preschooler about what the rainbow means; that God saved Noah and his family from the flood, and that God has promised never to flood the whole earth again.

RECOMMENDED READING

Do you want to pass faith and character to your children?
A great short book on this topic is "Family Worship," by Don Whitney.

Genesis 11:1–9

The Tower of Babel

Activity

Words in **bold** are what you can say to lead this activity.

Supplies needed: Whatever you decide to use

To get our family worship time started tonight, we are going to have a competition. Every person will be on their own, except for little ones who can find a partner. I wonder who will win? I wonder who will be the best? Well, let's find out. The competition is this. Who can build the highest tower? I am going to give us our building materials, and each of us has to build the highest tower possible. The one who has the highest tower at the end of the time is the winner. He or she will be the best.

You have a lot of choices with what to use for building materials, so be creative. You could try: coins, laundry, books, Lego, shoes, or really anything people want. Note: Avoid things that might hurt someone if the tower falls! Once you have determined what building materials will be allowed, you can begin!

OK, I think we are ready to start. I am going to give you a maximum of five minutes to complete your tower. If it falls while you are building it, rebuild as fast as you can. When the time is up...the time is up... and our champion will be crowned. Begin!

When the time is up ask the winner to stand up, perhaps even stand on a stool or chair in front of the family. Give them a chance to bow, while the rest of the family applauds.

You all did a great job building your towers. Of course we had a winner, and we made a big deal about it. How did it feel to win? How did it feel to stand up and have everyone applaud for you? What about the rest of us...those of us that didn't win? How did it feel to lose? How did it feel to not be the one to stand up and be recognized?

Even in a little game like this, feelings of pride can creep into our hearts. Feelings of jealousy and sadness can be there as well. In a few minutes we are going to open the Bible and read about a historical event with a real tower...and real pride.

Singing

Consider one or more of the following songs to praise God for His creation. Use the resources in the introduction to find music and lyrics for suggested songs.

Walk in His Ways, by Seeds Family Worship

All Creatures of our God and King

Shout to the Lord

Scripture Reading: Genesis 11:1–9

Read the above Scriptures aloud as a family. If time is short for your family worship time, skip other sections, not this one!

Talk About It

Discuss the following questions as a family. The brief answers provided may help you guide the conversation as needed.

1. **Have you ever wondered how all the different languages of the world came to be? In the passage we just read, God gives us the true history of how different languages began. How would you describe what happened?**
   Up until this time, all of Noah's descendants spoke one language. However, because of the pride and disobedience of the people at the tower of Babel, God caused different groups to begin speaking different languages. These people then gathered together in their language groups and began to spread out around the earth.

2. **In verse 4, we learn that the people in Shinar did two things that were against God. What was the first one?** The text says, "Come, let us build ourselves a city and a tower with its top in the heavens, and let us make a name for ourselves." The first sin of the people at Babel was pride. They wanted to be famous! Talk as a family about how you see people seeking fame today.

3. **The second sin is harder to find, but it is also found in verse 4. Can anyone see it?** The verse tells us that the people were fearful of being "dispersed over the face of the whole earth." What was the first commandment that God gave to Adam and Eve, and then again to Noah's family? "Be fruitful, multiply, and fill the earth." God wanted the earth filled with people for His glory, but the people of Babel wanted to stay where they were, and were therefore disobeying His direct command.

4. **God continues to call His people to action! He calls us to reach out every day to show love to our family members and to our neighbors. More than that, God wants His people thinking about reaching the whole world for Christ. How might God be calling our family to take the focus off ourselves, and work together to make a difference in the world for Christ?** It may help to break this conversation into categories. Talk about what it would mean to grow as a family in serving each other and helping each other grow spiritually. From there, talk about how God may be calling your family into deeper ministry in the church. Then talk about the opportunities God may be giving you in your neighborhood, in the nation, and in the world.

Prayer

A powerful way to pray as a family is to follow the "ACTS" model. You may choose to pray through one or all of these sections. Invite anyone who wants to pray to do so.

ADORATION

In reading the Bible today, what are some of the things that we learned about God? *(He is holy. He brings judgment against sin. He wants the world filled with worship.)* **Let's begin our prayer time by worshipping God for these things.**

CONFESSION

The people of Shinar were prideful, and they did not confess it. They wanted to "stay" when God wanted them to "go." This is an opportunity for us to confess our sins to God. *It is important that a parent begin this time of confession. Kids need to see parents set the example of how to humbly admit and confess sin.*

THANKSGIVING

God brought blessing out of rebellion at Babel. He created new languages and new people groups. Thank God for the ways that He has taken difficult situations in your family and turned them for good.

SUPPLICATION

The God of the Universe invites us to share our needs and requests with Him. Like a loving Father, He loves to bless us. Let's ask God for the things we need.

A parent can conclude the family worship time with a prayer of thanks to God.

Growing Together Throughout the Week

Keep the conversation about God and His Word going throughout the week. Consider talking about some of these questions at meal times, in the car, or before bed. Some brief answers are provided to help you guide the conversation.

1. **The people at Babel tried to build a tower "with its top in the heavens." They wanted to be like God and rule the Earth. Can you think of ways that people today try to make themelves "larger than life?"**
   Talk about stories of people who became so "full of themselves" that they came to ruin. You might talk about historical leaders like Napoleon or Hitler, or athletes like Barry Bonds and Tiger Woods.

2. **If you had to guess, how many languages do you think are spoken in the world today?**
    Visit https://www.wycliffe.org/about/why and look up the answer.
    There are about 7,000 languages spoken in the world.

3. **Out of all those different languages, how many do you think do not have the Bible in their own language?**
    There are 1,600 languages with no Bible translation. Spend some time as a family going through the Wycliffe website. Talk about ways you can help them get God's Word to every family in the world.

4. **The basic sin at the tower of Babel was pride. Some have suggested that pride is the sin behind every other sin. What do you think about that? Do you think that everything we do wrong has something to do with pride?**
    Talk about what pride looks like in your family. Do some people struggle with bragging? Do others struggle with selfishness? Are there insults and sarcasm? It is one thing to say "we struggle with pride," but another thing to identify specific prideful behaviors and then work to end them. Close this discussion time by praying for humility in your home.

Family Memory Verse

Work together as a family to memorize this verse this week.

And God blessed them. And God said to them, "Be fruitful and multiply and fill the earth and subdue it, and have dominion over the fish of the sea and over the birds of the heavens and over every living thing that moves on the earth." (Genesis 1:28)

Catechism Questions

As you go through your week, help each other learn the answers to these important questions. You may choose to include catechism as a part of your family worship time.

15. **Who wrote the Bible?** Holy men who were taught by the Holy Spirit.

16. **Who were our first parents?** Adam and Eve.

17. **Of what were our first parents made?** God made the body of Adam out of the ground, and made Eve out of one of Adam's ribs.

Digging Deeper—For Teens

There is strong evidence that the ruins of the tower of Babel still exist today. Use the steps below to do your own research, and draw your own conclusions.

1. Open your Bible to Genesis 10:9–10. Get a piece of paper and write down the name of the first great ruler of the land of Shinar (also known as Sumer).

2. Go forward to Genesis 11:2. Write down where the tower of Babel was built.

3. We know that the tower was not completed, and was abandoned because God confused the language of the people. However, this is not the last time that history mentions this tower. In 605BC (more than 1,500 years after the tower was originally built), King Nebuchadnezzar of Babylon wrote an inscription about his detailed plans to rebuild the tower. You can find a translation of Nebuchadnezzar's inscription by searching the internet for "Most ancient monument of Babylon." This will give you many citations of what Nebuchadnezzar said about this tower.

4. Write down all the ways that Nebuchadnezzar's writings agree with what the Bible says in Genesis 11.

5. Nebuchadnezzar identifies a particular location where the tower was built. The city of Borsippa, which is located in modern day Iraq.

6. Use Google maps or another satellite mapping program, (or a book that has photographs of the ruins of the towers, pyramids, and ziggurats of the ancient world) and search for "Borsippa, Iraq." What do you see?

7. Finally, go to **Wikipedia.com,** search for "Borsippa" and read the first paragraph.

Preschool Fun

Take a few moments and think of any words that you may know from a foreign language. See if you can teach your preschooler five foreign language words and what they mean in English. Talk with your preschooler about how God chose to fill the world with different languages, and that God knows all of them. People from all over the world are praying to God right now, in thousands of languages, and God is listening!

Genesis 11:27–12:20

God Calls Abraham

Activity

Words in **bold** are what you can say to lead this activity.

Supplies needed:

> None needed—but pictures or sports cards of famous athletes may help.

I want to ask you all a question. Who is the best professional athlete you can think of? You may choose to stick with one sport. **OK, let's stick with that sport. Can someone name another famous player?** Come up with a list of names. Give everyone a chance. Parents can help the little ones. **We have a list of great players here...but which one is the best of the best? Who would you choose?** Let each person "nominate" the player they think is the very best. Feel free to have the same brief conversation about other sports.

For added fun, try and find pictures, sports cards, magazines, or newspaper articles that talk about these athletes. You may encourage smaller children to draw a picture of one of the athletes playing the sport.

Does anyone know where the best players from each sport "go" when they retire? The answer is that they go to a place called "The Hall of Fame." These are huge museums where they have posters, statues, videos, and memorabilia that celebrate the players greatest acheivements.

Sports can be really fun. Unfortunately, we live in a culture where people become heros because they can put a ball through a metal hoop, or throw a football into the endzone. Do you think God is impressed by people who can jump high or run fast? What things does God care about?

There is a chapter in the Bible, Hebrews 11, that some people call "The Hall of Faith." It tells the stories of some of the most faithful people in the Scriptures. Let's go to Hebrews 11 and find as many names as we can.

During the next few weeks of family worship we are going to learn about one of these people from "The Hall of Faith." His name is Abraham.

Singing

Consider one or more of the following songs to praise God for how He leads and directs our lives. Use the resources in the introduction to find music and lyrics for suggested songs.

Never be Shaken, by Seeds Family Worship

Trust and Obey

I Am, by David Crowder

Scripture Reading: Genesis 11:27–12:20

Read the above Scriptures aloud as a family. Encourage different family members to read the Scriptures.

Talk About It

Discuss the following questions as a family. The brief answers provided may help you guide the conversation as needed. Feel free to change and adapt the questions as needed. See where God will take your conversation!

1. **What we just read is one of the most important events in the Bible. God chose this man, Abram, whom we know as Abraham, to believe in Him and follow Him. What was the first thing God asked Abram to do?** He asked him to leave his father's household and go to a new land, a land that God would show him.

2. **God also made a promise to Abram. What was it? Look at Genesis 12:2–3.** God promised Abram that 1) He would make him into a great

nation, 2) He would bless him, 3) Abram's name would be great, and 4) all the people of earth would be blessed through him. God called Abram to a global mission.

3. **God promised Abram that his descendants would bless the earth. What was hard to believe about that promise?** Abram had no children and his wife Sarai was barren. Read Genesis 15:1–6 to find out whether or not Abram chose to believe God. This is an example of how God called Abram to a faith mission.

4. **What did Abram do with his family? Did God call him to go to the new land on his own?** Abram took his family with him. He left with his wife, his nephew Lot, Lot's family, and his household servants. God called Abram to a family mission.

5. **We also read about a terrible situation when Abram and Sarai went to Egypt. Why was it wrong for Abram to go to Egypt in the first place?** God told him to go to a land He would show him. But there was a famine, Abram was scared, and he did not trust God to provide for him.

6. **Abram did not trust God when he went to Egypt. He also did not trust that God would protect them in Egypt. What did he do?** He lied about who Sarai was, and made Sarai lie as well.

7. **Having faith in God means telling the truth at all costs. Truthfulness is one of the best tests of how much a person trusts God. Are there**

times when you are tempted to lie? How can we help each other as a family to be more truthful? Parents, this is a good opportunity for you to share a story about a time you lied. Tell your family why you lied, and the consequences that came from it.

Prayer

A powerful way to pray as a family is to follow the "ACTS" model. You may choose to pray through one or all of these sections. Invite anyone who wants to pray to do so.

ADORATION

In reading the Bible today, what are some of the things that we learned about God? *(He leads us. He talks to us. He makes promises to us).* **Let's begin our prayer time by worshipping God for these things.**

CONFESSION

Abram and Sarai struggled to trust God to provide for them. They lied rather than trust God to protect them in Egypt. Let's take some time now and confess to God our struggles in trusting Him. We can also confess to God lies that we have told. Just as God was gracious with Abraham and Sarai, He will be gracious with us.

THANKSGIVING

God has been blessing the world through Abraham's descendants for 4,000 years. As followers of Jesus, we are spiritual heirs of Abraham and share in that same blessing! Let's thank God for keeping His promises.

SUPPLICATION

The God of the Universe invites us to share our needs and requests with Him. Like a loving Father, He loves to bless us. Let's ask God for the things we need.

A parent can conclude the family worship time with a prayer of thanks to God.

Growing Together Throughout the Week

Keep the conversation about God and His Word going throughout the week. Consider talking about some of these questions at meal times, in the car, or before bed. Some brief answers are provided to help you guide the conversation.

1. **God made promises to Abram. God always keeps His promises. Have you ever made a promise that you didn't keep? Has someone ever**

made a promise to you that they did not keep? How did it make you feel?

2. **When the famine came to the land, Abram was scared. He did not trust God and he went to Egypt. There, he lied because he did not trust God to protect him. Why do you think people tell lies?**
There are two big reasons people lie: 1) To get stuff, and 2) To get out of stuff. We lie to get things we want, such as money, or toys, or the approval of others. We also lie to get out of trouble and avoid consequences. Try to lead the conversation in such a way that family members feel safe to admit their struggles with lying, and to admit lies that they have told. Everyone has lied! God knows all our lies and He still loves us. Use this time to create an environment of grace and forgiveness.

3. **How do you think Abram felt leaving his homeland without knowing exactly where he was going? All he knew is that God would show him where to go. How would you feel?**
Abram was probably scared. He had a wife and a large household to take care of. How would he provide? Would they be safe? Where would they end up? God often calls families on bold adventures to advance His Kingdom. Might God be calling your family on a bold adventure?

Family Memory Verse

Work together as a family to memorize this verse this week.

"For I have chosen him, that he may command his children and his household after him to keep the way of the LORD by doing righteousness and justice, so that the LORD may bring to Abraham what he has promised him." (Genesis 18:19)

Catechism Questions

As you go through your week, help each other learn the answers to these important questions. You may choose to include catechism as a part of your family worship time.

In the last three weeks you have worked on nine new questions. Take time this week to review the past questions. Can anyone in the family answer all 17 questions you have studied so far?

Digging Deeper—For Teens

Consider having some of the following conversations with your teenager this week.

1. Have you ever made a promise and kept it? Have you ever made a promise, but failed to keep it? How should it affect our daily lives that God always keeps His promises?

2. In what ways do you see people around you lie: either to get what they want, or to get out of trouble? Do you think people generally see lying as a serious thing or something that is no big deal?

3. In your opinion, what is the number one reason why a teenager might tell a lie?

4. God called Abram when he was very old. But many times in the Bible God calls people when they are very young. Have you begun to sense God calling you into a specific mission for Him and for His Kingdom?

5. God gave Abraham a multi-generational vision long before he even had children of his own. Although it may seem a long way off now, God will likely bless you with children someday, and you are not too young to be thinking about them and what it will take to raise them to know and love God. What character trait do you believe you most need to work on in order to be a godly father or mother someday?

Preschool Fun

If you did not already sing a rousing rendition of "Father Abraham," your preschooler will love it! The more you put into it, the more he or she will enjoy it. If there are older siblings in the house, encourage them to take the lead.

PUT IT ON THE CALENDAR

One of the reasons why family worship is so hard is because of our crazy schedules.

If we say, "Let's do family worship tonight if we have time," that probably means, "We are not doing family worship tonight." You will have more success by talking together as a family about a specific time that you will plan on meeting for family worship. "Tonight, let's try and meet together at 7pm for family worship, OK?" Things may come up and it may not happen right at 7pm, or it may not even happen at all, but if you plan on a specific time you will be more likely to make it happen!

Genesis 16:1–18:15

Abraham and Sarah Doubt God

Activity

Words in **bold** are what you can say to lead this activity.

Supplies needed:

Something yummy that you can serve as a special dessert or snack. Keep it out of sight.

We are going to have a great time at family worship tonight. I want to begin by making you a promise. I have something that I know that you are all going to enjoy. We have a special dessert/snack tonight. In a few minutes, we are all going to be able to enjoy it together! Let me tell you about it.

Describe the food that you will be eating. Make it sound as appealing as possible. For instance, "We will have hand-scooped vanilla ice cream. Each person will be able to choose their own gourmet topping. Options will include Oreos, M & M's, sprinkles and whipped cream."

What do you all think? Raise your hand if you think my idea for this special treat is a good plan. I promise that we are going to all enjoy this together. How many of you would like to have your treats now? (Be prepared for cheers here!)

I don't blame you. It is going to taste really good. But I have decided that we are going to save all the treats for after family worship. We will all get to practice a little patience.

It is hard to wait for things, isn't it? It is going to be hard to wait for our dessert. Can you think of other things that are hard to wait for?

Encourage everyone in the family to share a response to this question.

When we open the Bible in a few minutes, we are going to read about Abraham and Sarah. God promised they would have a son. They waited and waited. They had a choice whether they would continue to believe God or doubt His promises. We will find out what happens.

Singing

Consider one or more of the following songs to praise God for His faithfulness. Use the resources in the introduction to find music and lyrics for suggested songs.

Sing Praise to Him, by Seeds Family Worship

Even So Come, by Travis Cottrell

Great is Thy Faithfulness

Scripture Reading: Genesis 16:1–18:15

The Scripture reading for this week is longer than usual. Consider having different family members read different sections or plan on breaking up the reading into two or more times of family worship.

Part of this passage includes God's instruction to Abraham to circumcise the males in his household. This may bring up conversations about issues of sexuality. Consider using *The Child's Story Bible* by Catherine Vos as an excellent resource for communicating God's truth from this passage in a way that children can understand.

Talk About It

Discuss the following questions as a family. The brief answers provided may help you guide the conversation as needed.

1. **In our last time of family worship we learned that God promised He would not only give Abraham a son, but many, many descendants as well. However, time passed and Abraham's wife Sarai still was not pregnant. What did she do?** She asked her servant Hagar to try to have a baby with Abraham. Unfortunately, Abraham agreed with this plan. (You may need to remind the family that when we first meet Abraham's wife her name is Sarai, but God later changes her name to Sarah.)

2. **Instead of coming up with their own plan, what should Abraham and Sarai have done?** They should have trusted God, believed His promise, and waited for Him to do what He said he would do.

3. **Even though Abraham and Sarah doubted God, God remained faithful to them. Look again at Genesis 17:6–7. Does anyone know what a covenant is?** A covenant is an agreement or a contract. In this case, God made an agreement with Abraham. God announced to Abraham that He was going to use Abraham's descendants to bless the world.

4. **God pushed Abraham to focus on his (as yet unborn) children, grandchildren and great-grandchildren. How can our family be a blessing for generations to come?** This is an opportunity to talk about how all the decisions that we make in our families today leave a legacy for our grandchildren and great grandchildren yet to be born. God's desire is that our faith would be a multi-generational faith. God's desire is that "our ceiling would be our children's floor." In other words, we want our children to love God more than we have, know the Bible better than we do, and carry the Gospel further than we can.

5. **Sarah laughed when she heard the angel tell Abraham that she would have a son in her old age (Genesis 18:12). This was not the first time she heard the promise, but still she did not believe it. What are some ways that we struggle to believe what God has said?** The world pressures us to laugh at what God has said in the Bible. People

laugh at the idea that God created the world. People laugh at the truth that Jesus rose again from the dead. People laugh at the idea that Jesus is coming back to judge the world. Every Christian struggles with doubts. This is a good opportunity for your family to share your doubts with each other, and ask God to strengthen your faith. Doubt your doubts! Believe your beliefs!

Prayer

A powerful way to pray as a family is to follow the "ACTS" model. You may choose to pray through one or all of these sections. Invite anyone who wants to pray to do so.

ADORATION

In reading the Bible today, what are some of the things that we learned about God? *(He keeps His promises. He speaks to us. He cares for our children, grandchildren and great grandchildren).* **Praise God for these things!**

CONFESSION

We all struggle with doubt. God welcomes us when we express our doubts and lack of faith to Him.

THANKSGIVING

How has God kept His promises to your family? How has God blessed the generations of your family? Thank Him for these things now.

SUPPLICATION

Do you need more faith? Ask God for it. Do you have family members who don't know God? Pray for them now.

A parent can conclude the family worship time with a prayer of thanks to God.

Growing Together Throughout the Week

Keep the conversation about God and His Word going throughout the week. Consider talking about some of these questions at meal times, in the car, or before bed. Some brief answers are provided to help you guide the conversation.

1. **Abraham and Sarah wanted to have children very badly. But they were not patient and they did not wait for God. What bad things happened because they did not wait for God?**

Hagar and Sarai began to hate each other, and it caused problems between Abraham and Sarai. When we choose to do things our own way, rather than God's way, other people in our families are often hurt.

2. **What was the name of the son that was born to Hagar? What did God say would happen to him?**
His name was Ishmael. He is considered to be the father of the Muslim faith. In Genesis 16:12 it says that Ishmael's life would be filled with conflict and violence.

3. **How old were Abraham and Sarah when she conceived?**
Genesis 17:17 says that Abraham was 100 years old, and Sarah was 90. It would have to be a true miracle for them to have a child since Sarah was past the age that women can have babies.

4. **Look at Genesis 18:14. There is a powerful question there. "Is anything too hard for the Lord?" Are you facing things in your life right now that are so hard that they seem impossible? In light of this verse, what should we do?**
Is anything too hard for the Lord? No! We can take all of our pain and problems to Him. We can trust Him to work everything together for good if we love Him.

Family Memory Verse

Work together as a family to memorize this verse this week.

"Is anything too hard for the Lord?" (Genesis 18:14)

Catechism Questions

As you go through your week, help each other learn the answers to these important questions. You may choose to include catechism as a part of your family worship time.

18. **In what condition did God make Adam and Eve?** He made them holy and happy.

19. **What is Sin?** Sin is any disobedience to God's Law.

20. **What does every sin deserve?** The wrath and curse of God.

Digging Deeper—For Teens

Consider having some of the following conversations with your teenager this week:

1. God did not bless Abraham with his son Isaac until 13 years after Ishmael was born. This was a major test of Abraham's faith and patience. Do you ever feel like God is testing your faith? If so, how? Share some big prayers you are still waiting for God to answer.

2. In Genesis 18:1-2, the Bible says that the LORD appeared to Abraham, but the next verse says that Abraham saw three men. Later, in chapter 19, two of the "men" are in fact revealed to be angels who then strike the cities of Sodom and Gomorrah. Many Bible scholars believe that the third "man" that Abraham saw was Jesus Christ, making an appearance here in the Old Testament. What do you think? Do some research on this topic with your parents.

3. A major focus of the Abraham and Sarah story is the importance of marriage and children. Has God given you a desire for marriage and children? What are some steps can you take now to prepare yourself to be a godly spouse and parent when you get older?

4. God worked a miracle when He enabled Abraham and Sarah to conceive a child. Do you believe God works miracles today? Why/why not? Share a time where God answered one of your prayers.

5. In Genesis 16:12, we find a prophesy about Ishmael, the father of the Muslim religion. Muslims claim that the Bible was altered to reflect poorly on Ishmael and to make it look like Isaac was the son of the covenant. Do some research on how Christians can make a difference in the lives of Muslims. Go to **www.breakpoint.org** and type "Islam" in the search box to find a variety of thought provoking articles.

Preschool Fun

Have a contest with your preschooler about who can "freeze" the longest. Who can stand on one leg, perfectly still the longest? Who can stare without blinking the longest? Who can hold a "silly face" the longest without laughing? Talk with your son or daughter about how sometimes God wants us to "be still" and wait for Him to answer our prayers. God promises that Jesus will come back one day. He wants us to believe Him and wait. If we want to love God, it means being patient with Him and with one another.

Genesis 18:16–19:29
God Destroys Sodom and Gomorrah

Activity

Words in **bold** are what you can say to lead this activity. Supplies needed: Just stuff you already have around the house.

To get our family worship time started tonight, I need a volunteer. Have the volunteer stand up and move into a part of the room where they have some space.

Thanks for volunteering. We need you to pretend that you are an old-fashioned scale. Have you ever seen one of those before? I am not talking about the kind of scale that you stand on and it tells you how much you weigh. If you are going to be an old-fashioned scale, I need you to put your arms out to the sides, completely straight. Now put your palms up toward the ceiling. We are going to put different things in your hands, and it is going to be your job to tell us which side is heavier and which side is lighter.

Here is where the rest of us come in. Everyone needs to go find three different objects. Each object should be able to be held in one hand. Try not to pick anything that will break or hurt someone if it falls. Give people some time to find their three objects.

OK, volunteer, it is time to begin. We need you to close your eyes. We are going to come up and put one object in each of your hands, and you need to 1) guess what is in your hand and 2) tell us which object (right hand or left hand) is heavier. You can do a few rounds of this, and let different people volunteer to be the scale.

Now, we are going to do this a little differently. Stand up again, put your arms out, and close your eyes. We are going to try to pile all of our objects in one of your hands, even piling them on your arm if we have to. Let's see what happens. See if you can hold everything! As you pile the objects on one side of the "scale" eventually that arm will begin to sag and get tired. The scale will "tip" toward the weight.

The reason that we did this game is because it gives us a picture of what we will read about in the Bible. We are going to read about the cities of Sodom and Gomorrah, and how the sin in these cities became so terrible that it outweighed any good that was there. As a result, the scales of God's judgment fell against these cities, and God destroyed them. It is a serious part of the Bible and God has a lot for us to learn.

Singing

Consider one or more of the following songs to praise God for His faithfulness. Use the resources in the introduction to find music and lyrics for suggested songs.

Out of the Mud, by Seeds Family Worship

A Mighty Fortress is our God

Days of Elijah

Scripture Reading: Genesis 18:16–19:29

Read the above Scripture out loud as a family. This is a dramatic, serious and sad series of events.

Be warned—this passage will bring up challenging issues about sin, judgment, and sexuality. Consider using *The Child's Story Bible* by Catherine Vos as an excellent resource to help you communicate God's truth from this passage. However, at the same time, don't feel the need to shield your children from the difficult issues presented in God's word. The world bombards them daily with violence, disturbing images and sexual content. God created your family as a safe place for your children to learn the truth about these important things from His Word.

Talk About It

Discuss the following questions as a family. The brief answers provided may help you guide the conversation as needed.

1. **In the beginning of our reading, we learn something very important about God's call on Abraham's life. In verse 18, God tells Abraham, "all the nations on the earth will be blessed through him." Wow! God will use Abraham to impact the whole world. According to verse 19, what specifically did God call Abraham to do?** God called Abraham to direct "his children and his household after him to keep the way of the Lord." Abraham's most important ministry was to lead his family to follow God. God's mission for him was not a personal or individual mission, but a multi-generational mission. Christian families today are part of the same mission that God gave to Abraham 4000 years ago. It is our first and most important ministry to pass faith in God through the generations of our family.

2. **The LORD told Abraham that He had decided to destroy the cities of Sodom and Gomorrah. The scales had tipped against them, so to speak. But Abraham pleaded with the LORD to spare the city for the sake of the righteous who lived there (including his nephew Lot). What did Abraham ask the LORD and how did He respond?** Abraham asked the LORD if He would still destroy the cities if there were 50 righteous people there. The LORD said that He would not destroy the cities if there were 50 righteous people there. Abraham

then asked, well how about 40? No. 30? No. 20? No. 10? No. The only people who believed in God in both these cities were Lot and his family. God judges nations with the "scales." When evil completely outweighs good, then God brings judgment.

3. **When the angels arrived in Sodom, Lot insisted that they come and stay at his house. He did not know, at first, that they were angels. Soon all the men of the city, young and old, surrounded Lot's house and wanted to hurt the men. What did Lot do next?** Lot went outside to try and stop the mob from taking the men out of his house. This seemed like a brave thing to do. But Lot then did a very evil thing. He told the mob that they could have his two precious daughters, and that they could hurt them if they left the men alone. You may choose to take this opportunity to talk with your children about one of the fundamental sins of Sodom and Gomorrah: homosexuality. Or just talk with your children about God's awesome gift of marriage, and emphasize that God created sex only to be shared between one man and one woman in marriage.

4. **Lot did not trust God. He had been watching and listening to the sin around him for many years. He knew God, but because He did not separate his heart from his culture, and because he continued to watch the evil around him, in this situation he acted even worse than the men of Sodom. After Lot offered the crowd his daughters, what did the angels do?** They struck the entire mob with blindness, pulled Lot back into the house, and shut the door. Even though Lot had done a terrible thing, God was gracious to him. He showed him

107

mercy. Then the angels commanded Lot and his family to leave the city immediately so that they would not die.

5. **The angels gave Lot and his family specific instructions. Don't stop! Don't look back! But what did Lot's wife do, and what happened to her? How are we sometimes like Lot's wife?** Lot's wife, who was behind Lot, looked back, and she was turned into a pillar of salt. God wanted Lot and his family to leave all the evil of Sodom behind them. Unfortunately, our hearts can easily love the things of this world as well. Talk openly as a family about the things in this world (and in our culture) that tempt your heart away from God.

Prayer

For your prayer time today, consider using the "High-Low" prayer approach. You can use the words **in bold** below to help guide you.

Today in our prayer time I would like us to do "High-Low." To start, I would like to see if each person would be willing to share a "high," or a best part, of their day (or week) today. Encourage as many people in the family to share their high points.

Thank you all for sharing those things. Would someone be willing to pray and thank God and give Him praise for all the blessings that were just shared? If no one is comfortable praying, you can take the lead and thank God for the "highs" that were shared.

Now, would someone be willing to tell us about a "low" from today or from this week? What was the worst part of your day/week? It is helpful for you to go first when sharing "lows." Listen to each person share their lows with the family.

Thank you all for sharing those things. It is so important for us to open our hearts to each other. Would someone be willing to pray and ask God to help us with all the things we just heard? God loves us and we can bring everything to Him. If no one is comfortable praying, you can lead this time of prayer, asking God to help each person in your family as they face difficult situations.

Growing Together Throughout the Week

Keep the conversation about God and His Word going throughout the week. Consider talking about some of these questions at meal times, in the car, or before bed. Some brief answers are provided to help you guide the conversation.

1. **When you think of God destroying these two cities of Sodom and Gomorrah, how does it make you feel?**
    We often have mixed feelings of sadness for those who died, doubts about God's fairness, awe in response to God's power, and humility as we recognize how serious sin is.

2. **In 2 Peter 2:7–8 we learn that Lot spent far too much time looking at and listening to the evil things that were going on in Sodom. Today, we see and hear a lot of evil things on the TV and in movies. What should we do as a family to keep our eyes and ears from evil?**
Use this opportunity to talk as a family about setting godly boundaries around TV, internet, movies, and music.

3. **Even though Lot did a terrible thing by failing to protect his daughters, God showed him mercy. The angels pulled him back into the house. The angels led his family out of the city. Does God show His mercy like that to us?**
Yes, every day! We receive the mercy of God every time we sin. Talk about how amazing it is that because of God's great love for us, He became a man in Jesus Christ to take our sins upon Himself. He died in our place so that we might live. If we have put our faith in Jesus, we can know with absolute certainty that we are saved and that we will spend eternity with God.

Family Memory Verse

Work together as a family to memorize this verse this week.

"For God has not destined us for wrath, but to obtain salvation through our Lord Jesus Christ." (1 Thessalonians 5:9)

Catechism Questions

As you go through your week, help each other learn the answers to these important questions. You may choose to include catechism as a part of your family worship time.

21. What was the sin of our first parents? Eating the forbidden fruit.

22. Who tempted them to this sin? Satan tempted them.

23. What happened to our first parents when they had sinned? Instead of being holy and happy, they became sinful and miserable.

Digging Deeper—For Teens

Talk about these questions with your teen:

1. Sodom and Gomorrah are two cities that exemplify the biblical truth that when a nation's sin rises to a certain point, God brings judgment. What do you think about the idea that God might bring judgment against America if our sins continue to increase?

2. In the city of Sodom, every man, young and old, was a part of the crowd wanting to have sexual relations with the men inside of Lot's home. The mob was also angry at Lot for "judging" them. How are Christians today accused of "judging" those struggling with homosexuality? What pressures do you feel from your friends or classmates at school to affirm homosexuality?

3. What does the Bible teach about homosexuality? Use a study Bible or go to **www.biblegateway.com** to find all the references in Scripture to homosexuality. You may also want to read the excellent short book, *"What Does the Bible Really Teach About Homosexuality,"* by Kevin DeYoung. How does the culture usually present Christian attitudes regarding homosexuality? How does the Bible say we should treat others?

Specifically for young men:

4. Lot did not act like a godly man when he failed to protect his daughters, and when he failed to protect his wife. One of the true marks of a Christian man is that he protects the women in his life—his mother, sisters, wife and daughters. Even now as a young man, before you are married, how might you grow in this important area of lovingly and sacrificially caring for and protecting the women God has put in your family?

This final question is best addressed in private and whenever possible should be discussed between fathers and sons, and mothers and daughters.

5. Have you ever felt confusing feelings about your sexuality? Have you ever felt attraction for others of the same gender? These are important feelings to talk about. God created you to be attracted to the opposite sex. Satan loves to mix that up. Satan also wants you to hide your sexual thoughts and feelings from your parents. God wants

you to give your parents your heart and be honest with them about everything, even sexuality.

Preschool Fun

Sadly, these events do not lend themselves to much "preschool fun." It is important that our children see us responding to God's Word with proper joy and proper seriousness. This is a passage that demands more seriousness.

Genesis 21:1–21

God Keeps His Promise

Activity

Words in **bold** are what you can say to lead this activity.

Supplies needed: A lump of Play-Doh for each person OR a sheet of blank paper and something to write with for each person. The activity below will be written assuming you have Play-Doh. Adjust as needed.

I need everyone's help to get our family worship time started. I am going to give each of you a lump of Play-Doh.

Give everyone some Play-Doh. If you don't have any, give everyone a piece of paper and something to write with.

Now, I'd like each of us to take our Play-Doh and make it into something that reminds us of a funny family story. When you think of the funny things that have happened to our family, what comes to mind? It might be a small thing, or

something that happened a long time ago. Do you have a family memory that makes you laugh? Turn your Play-Doh into something that reminds you of that story or that memory.

Give people time to transform their Play-Doh. If you are using paper, give people a chance to draw their picture. Little ones may need to partner up with older siblings or with a parent.

Let's share our stories! Who wants to go first? Tell us about what you made and share your story or your memory.

Enjoy reminiscing with each other.

Laughter is a gift from God. Laughter is going to be a big part of our Bible reading today. We are going to read about a family that God blessed with laughter.

Singing

Consider one or more of the following songs to praise God for His faithfulness. Use the resources in the introduction to find music and lyrics for suggested songs.

Your Faithfulness, by Seeds Family Worship

Good Good Father, by Chris Tomlin

By Faith, by Keith and Kristyn Getty

Scripture Reading: Genesis 21:1–21

Read the following Scripture out loud as a family. Does one person usually read the Bible during this time? Consider asking someone else to read today.

Talk About It

Discuss the following questions as a family. The brief answers provided may help you guide the conversation as needed.

1. **Take a look at Genesis 21:1. What are the two things God does in this verse?** First, the text says that the LORD "visited Sarah" (ESV) or, "was gracious to Sarah" (NIV). Second, the LORD did what He promised: He gave Sarah a son. God loves to be gracious with us. God loves to prove to us that His promises are true.

2. **Do you remember what Sarah did when she first heard the prophecy that she would have a son in her old age?** She laughed. She didn't think it was possible. It was not a laugh of joy, but more like snickering or sneering. Even though Sarah laughed and doubted God, God was gracious to her and fulfilled His promise. Sarah doubted, but God was faithful.

3. **What does the name Isaac mean?** Why do you think they gave him this name? Isaac means "laughter" or "he laughs." Sarah's first laughs were filled with doubt. Imagine how she and Abraham were laughing now with joy at the birth of their son!

4. **Unfortunately, the whole family was not laughing. What happened with Hagar and Ishmael?** Ishmael was upset that Isaac had been born. He wanted to be the child of the promise. He was making fun of the baby boy Isaac! Abraham's family was now in chaos and pain because he had not trusted God 14 years ago. God had wanted Abraham to wait for a son, but instead Abraham and Sarah had taken matters into their own hands, and now their sin was still causing problems some 14 years later! It got so bad that God directed Abraham to remove Hagar and Ishmael from the family. This was a very hard, sad situation, and one that would not have happened if Abraham and Sarah had trusted God.

5. **How did God provide for Hagar and Ishmael? What does this tell us about God's heart?** God heard the desperate cries of Hagar and Ishmael. He sent an angel to them and provided them with water, saving their lives. Our God loves to show mercy and He always keeps His promises (Read Genesis 17:20).

6. **God has made many promises to us in the Bible. Can you think of some of those promises? Which promise is the most exciting to you?** You can find hundreds of promises in the Bible just by typing "God's promises" into an internet search engine. Consider having each person in the family write down one of God's promises from the Bible on a 3x5 card. You can put those "promise cards" around the house to remind the family of God's promises throughout the week.

Prayer

A powerful way to pray as a family is to follow the "ACTS" model. You may choose to pray through one or all of these sections. Invite anyone who wants to pray to do so.

ADORATION

In reading the Bible today, what are some of the things that we learned about God? *(He keeps His promises. He is gracious. Even when we doubt Him, He is faithful. He is never "late", but always fulfills His promises at the perfect time).* **Praise God for these things!**

CONFESSION

We all struggle with doubt, just like Sarah did. God welcomes us when we express our doubts and lack of faith to Him. It is important to share our doubts with our family, and with God.

THANKSGIVING

How has God kept His promises to your family? How has God blessed the generations of your family? Thank Him for these things now.

SUPPLICATION

God encourages us to bring all of our needs and burdens to Him. Take this time to ask God for the desires of your heart. Pray for His help with the conflicts in your family. Pray for God to work in the hearts of your friends and family members who don't know Him.

A parent can conclude the family worship time with a prayer of thanks to God.

Growing Together Throughout the Week

Keep the conversation about God and His Word going throughout the week. Consider talking about some of these questions at meal times, in the car, or before bed. Some brief answers are provided to help you guide the conversation.

1. **God fulfilled His promise to Abraham and Sarah. How do you think that this miracle changed Abraham's and Sarah's faith in God?**
   This was one of the most important moments in Abraham's life. In our next time of family worship we are going to talk about how Abraham's faith would soon be tested. We will find out if he passes the test.

2. **The passage we read talked about how God displayed his grace by "visiting" Sarah and enabling her to conceive. What does it mean for God to be gracious to us? Can you think of ways God has been gracious to our family?**

   This may be an opportunity for you to talk about the difference between grace and mercy. Grace is receiving a gift and blessing we do not deserve. Mercy is when we do not receive a punishment that we do deserve.

3. **When we doubt God and do things our own way, other members of our family will sometimes get hurt. Thankfully, God gives us a way to deal with hurt and pain in our families. It is called forgiveness. We all do things that hurt each other. But what can we do then? God wants us to become experts at apologizing and asking for forgiveness when we do things wrong, and also to become experts at granting forgiveness when others hurt us. On a scale of 1–10, how well do you think our family does when it comes to apologizing and granting forgiveness?**

   If you identify this as a growth area, talk as a family about how you could grow and develop more "expertise" in forgiving one another when you do things wrong.

Family Memory Verse

Work together as a family to memorize this verse this week.

"The LORD visited Sarah as he had said, and the LORD did to Sarah as he had promised." (Genesis 21:1)

Catechism Questions

As you go through your week, help each other learn the answers to these important questions. You may choose to include catechism as a part of your family worship time.

24. **What effect did the sin of Adam have on all mankind?** All of mankind is born in a state of sin and misery.

25. **Can anyone go to heaven with this sinful nature?** No; our hearts must be changed before we can be fit for heaven.

26. **What is a change of heart called?** Regeneration.

Digging Deeper—For Teens

Use these questions as a way to engage your teenager in conversation this week.

1. A major part of the story of Abraham and Sarah has to do with their deep sadness because they were not able to have children. Abraham

and Sarah would have given everything they had for a child. Do you think couples today have this same love and desire for children? Why/why not? In what ways does our culture seem to imply children are more of a burden than a blessing?

2. The events with Hagar and Ishmael are hard to understand. Hagar was mistreated by Sarah. Ishmael had to leave his father when he was 14 years old. It is understandable that Ishmael would be jealous. Read Genesis 21:14–21. How did God provide for Hagar and Ishmael after they had been sent into the wilderness? What does this tell you about God?

3. Why did God choose to make His covenant with Isaac and not Ishmael? *God is sovereign. He rules everything and everyone in the universe, and He chooses what to do. We don't always understand God's choices. When we see God's choices, we then have a choice. Will we trust that God is doing the right thing, or will we doubt God and accuse Him of being unfair?*

4. Are there situations in your life where you feel that God has been unfair with you? How have you responded? Are you facing a choice right now between believing that God knows what is best for your life versus doubting Him and being angry with Him?

Preschool Fun

Abraham and Sarah named their new baby boy "Isaac." His name means "he laughs" or "laughter." Play the game "make you laugh" with your preschooler. Ask your preschooler to make a straight face. No smiling. No frowning. See how long he or she can keep a straight face while you try to make him or her laugh. Then do it the other way. See how long you can keep a straight face while your child tries to make you laugh.

Genesis 22:1–19

God Tests Abraham

Activity

Words in **bold** are what you can say to lead this activity.

Supplies needed: Paper and pencil (for keeping score of the game).

I am sorry to say this, but during family worship today we are going to have to take a test. Don't panic! Hopefully it will be a fun test, if there is such a thing! Here is how it is going to work. Each one of us will have the chance to make up questions that we will ask the rest of the family. If anyone gets the question right, that person earns a point. I'll keep track of the points as we go.

You can ask any kind of question that you want. It might be a True/False question or a question about the Bible. It could be a personal question like, "What is my favorite color?" It might be a question about something that you have recently learned in class. The first family member to get it right would get a point.

Another way to do this game is to divide the family up into two teams. Teams go back and forth asking the other team questions, trying to stump them. If a team answers the question correctly, they get a point.

Are we ready to start? I am going to ask the family the first question. After that, the person on my right will get a chance to ask the next question, and we will go around until everyone has had a chance. Remember you get points for correctly answering someone else's questions. Ready?

Let the game begin! You will have fun coming up with questions, getting them right, and stumping each other. When you are done, announce the winner.

That was fun. Everyone knows what it is like to take a test. Tests can make us nervous. Passing feels great! Failing feels terrible. Teachers and parents are not the only ones who give us tests. God gives us tests too. In the Bible passage we are going to read today, we will learn about a time that God gave someone a very difficult test.

Singing

Consider one or more of the following songs to praise God for His goodness. Use the resources in the introduction to find music and lyrics for suggested songs.

Convinced, by Seeds Family Worship

Step by Step, by Rich Mullins

I Will Follow, by Jon Guerra

Scripture Reading: Genesis 22:1-19

Read the above Scripture out loud as a family. Does one person usually read the Bible during this time? Consider asking someone else to read today.

Talk About It

Discuss the following questions as a family. The brief answers provided may help you guide the conversation as needed.

1. **In Genesis 22:1, what does God do to Abraham?** God tests him. A teacher gives a student a test in order to help the student master the information. A test helps students build confidence that they know the material. This was a test to see how strong Abraham's faith was.

2. **God asked Abraham to do what seemed like a terrible thing. He told Him to sacrifice his dear son Isaac. What did Abraham do? The answer is in Genesis 22:3.** He rose up early the next morning, got the supplies ready, and set out on the journey with Isaac. He obeyed immediately. How do we do in our family at immediate obedience? Do we obey God quickly when we read the Bible? Do we obey parents quickly when they give us instructions?

3. **Once they arrived at Mount Moriah, Abraham tied up his son Isaac and laid him on the altar. Isaac did not struggle or fight back. What does that tell you about Isaac?** Abraham was demonstrating total

trust in God, his Heavenly Father, by obeying what God had told him to do. Isaac was demonstrating total trust in his earthly father, by doing what Abraham told him to do.

4. **What do you think Abraham was thinking? What was he thinking as they were walking to the mountain? What was he thinking as he tied up Isaac and put him on the altar?** Let the family share their responses and ideas. After some ideas are shared, invite someone to read Hebrews 11:17–19. God tells us what Abraham was thinking! Abraham was so convinced in God's promise that Isaac would be a great nation he figured that if God was asking him to kill Isaac, that God must have planned on raising Isaac from the dead. Amazing faith!

5. **God provided a lamb for Abraham to take the place of Isaac. How has God done the same thing for us?** We deserve to die because of our sins (Romans 6:23). But because of God's great love for us, He provided a substitute for us. God provided Jesus, "the Lamb of God, who takes away the sin of the world" (John 1:29). Read John 1:29–34. If there are members of your family who have not accepted Jesus' sacrifice for them on the cross, invite them to put their trust in Christ today.

Prayer

A powerful way to pray as a family is to follow the "ACTS" model. You may choose to pray through one or all of these sections. Invite anyone who wants to pray to do so.

ADORATION

In reading the Bible today, what are some of the things that we learned about God? *He cares about us enough to test us. He always provides for our needs. He loves it when we obey Him and believe in Him. Just like He provided a lamb to rescue Isaac, He provided Jesus to rescue all of us from sin. Praise God for these things!*

CONFESSION

God tests all of us. Unfortunately, many times we fail those tests. Unlike Abraham and Isaac we don't obey God and trust His Word. Confess your failures to each other, and to God.

THANKSGIVING

Let's take some time to thank God for Jesus! We deserve death for our sins, but God provided a perfect lamb, Jesus Christ, to die in our place.

SUPPLICATION

Let's pray for strength and faith. God will continue to bring tests into the life of our family. Ask Him to help us see the tests when they come, and to believe in what God has said in the Bible—no matter what.

A parent can conclude the family worship time with a prayer of thanks to God.

Growing Together Throughout the Week

Keep the conversation about God and His Word going throughout the week. Consider talking about some of these questions at meal times, in the car, or before bed. Some brief answers are provided to help you guide the conversation.

1. **If you were Isaac, do you think you would have obeyed your father?**
   Parents, this is a good opportunity for you to share about times you chose to disobey your parents when you were younger, or delayed in being obedient. You may also choose to talk with your children about how "delayed obedience" is not obedience that pleases God.

2. **Thankfully, God has never again tested someone like He tested Abraham. He will never ask us to do something like this. But God does test us. Can you think of a time that God gave you a test? Did you pass or fail?**
   Again, you may begin this conversation by sharing about times in your life that God has tested your faith. Sometimes we are faithful and obey. Other times we are faithless and disobey. Share openly with your child so he or she will learn to share openly with you.

3. **Abraham almost sacrificed Isaac on Mount Moriah. Did you know that Mount Moriah is in Jerusalem? In fact, the Jews built the temple on the exact place where this happened. Moreover, Jesus was**

crucified not far from this place. Sadly, just before 700AD, Muslims conquered Jerusalem and built a temple there called the Dome of the Rock. Go online or grab a history book off your shelf and learn more about all the amazing things that have happened on Mount Moriah.

Family Memory Verse

Work together as a family to memorize this verse this week.

The next day he saw Jesus coming toward him, and said, "Behold, the Lamb of God, who takes away the sin of the world!" (John 1:29)

Catechism Questions

During the past three weeks your family has learned the answers to 9 new questions. Use this time to review those questions. Can anyone in the family answer all nine correctly?

Digging Deeper—For Teens

Consider talking about these questions with your teen

1. In Genesis 22:11 we learn that "the angel of the LORD" stopped Abraham from sacrificing Isaac. This is no ordinary angel! Use ***www.biblegateway.com*** or a study Bible to search for "the angel of

the Lord." Look at Genesis 22:15 for a clue as to who this unique being might be. (Spoiler at the bottom of the page)

2. What parts of your faith are you completely confident in? What doubts do you have? God can handle our doubts. It is OK to be honest about them. One of the best things a teenager can do when they are doubting God is talk about those doubts with mom or dad. *(Spoiler: Many Bible scholars believe that "the angel of the Lord" is Jesus Christ Himself, the second person of the Trinity, working in and through history prior to the Incarnation. If you take the time to find the other places in the Bible where "the angel of the LORD" appears you will agree that this cannot be just an angel!)*

Preschool Fun

Teach your preschooler to do a "trust fall" with you. Have your preschooler stand up and turn around so he or she is looking away from you. Sit down or kneel close behind your child. You should be less than a foot away. Put your hands on your child's back and say, "Do you trust me? You can feel my hands on your back. I want you to fall backwards and trust me that I will catch you." Give your child a couple tries to get the hang of it. Then try it one time with your hands a few inches away. See if your child will have enough faith to fall back into your hands!

SUPERCHARGE YOUR FAMILY WORSHIP

Here are some ways to help your family worship times become more meaningful and consistent:

Set aside time for family worship on the calendar. If you don't plan it, other things may crowd it out.

1. **Guard your evening schedules.** If people are pulled in too many directions, too many nights a week, your family will pay a price. A family who is always on the go cannot grow!

2. **Encourage teenagers to take practice leading family worship.** In just a few years they may have children of their own and need to lead family worship in their own homes.

3. **Talk as a family about your "next step."** Are you currently praying together but not reading your Bible? Adding Bible reading is a good next step. Do you currently have one time of family worship each month? Your challenge might be moving to every week. What is the "next step" for your family?

Genesis 25:21–26, 27:1–45

God Chooses Jacob over Esau

Activity

Words in **bold** are what you can say to lead this activity.

> Supplies needed: A blindfold (a bandana works great). Family members may go and get other items as the activity unfolds, but nothing else is required to be on hand.

Let's start family worship today with a game. This is a game of disguises. I am going to need your best pretending skills. You might even need to play a little bit of a trick on someone. To get things started, I need a volunteer. I will need more people in a few minutes, but for now I just need one. It may work best to have a parent or older child be the first volunteer.

The first thing we need is for you to put on this blindfold. It is very important that you can't see anything. You are going to pretend to be a blind person— because we are going to read about a blind person in our Scripture reading in a few minutes. Once the person is all set with his or her blindfold...

You can't see anything right? Now the game begins. Each one of us is going to come up to you. We will offer you a part of our body to touch. We may offer you our head, our hand, or our arm. You have to figure out who it is, just by touching them. Be careful! We can try and trick you. We can put a blanket over our arm. We can put on something to use as a wig. Disguises are allowed! But there is no talking, and you can only touch the part of the person that they want you to touch. Who wants to go first? Let each person try to trick the person with the blindfold.

Now we are going to try this again. But we need a new volunteer.

This time we are going to make it a little more tricky. This time, you need to figure out who is standing next to you without talking or touching. All you can do is smell them! You can't even touch them with your nose...just smell. See if you can guess! Let each person in the family take a turn with the blindfold.

It can be hard to recognize who is with you if you can't see them. In our Bible passage today, we are going to read about a situation where this really happened.

Singing

Consider one or more of the following songs to praise God for His faithfulness. Use the resources in the introduction to find music and lyrics for suggested songs. Have you checked out SEEDS Family Worship resources? These great CDs and

DVDs will help your family enjoy the blessing of singing Scripture together. **www.seedsfamilyworship.net**

Grace, by Seeds Family Worship

Amazing Grace

Your Grace is Enough

Scripture Reading: Genesis 25:21–26; 27:1–45

The Scripture reading for this week is in two parts. Consider having different people read each section.

Talk About It

Discuss the following questions as a family. The brief answers provided may help you guide the conversation as needed.

1. **In our last time of family worship, we read about how God protected Isaac when he was a teenager. Now, Isaac is married to a woman named Rebekah, and he is 60 years old. God blessed them with twins growing inside Rebekah, and they were fighting with each other in her womb. Rebekah prayed and asked God to explain this to her. What did God tell her? (Gen 25:23)** God told her that "two nations," were growing within her. He also said (and this was surprising) that

the younger would serve the older. It was normal for the oldest son in the family to be the leader of the next generation. However, God told Rebekah that He had chosen the younger son to be the family leader.

2. **The second chapter we read takes place many years later. Isaac is about 137 years old. Jacob and Esau are over 70 years old. Isaac asks Esau, the older son, to prepare a meal for him and receive his father's blessing. This blessing meant that Esau would become the leader of the family after Isaac died. But what did Rebekah and Jacob do?** Rebekah planned a trick. She convinced Jacob, the younger brother, to lie to his father. Jacob pretended to be Esau, and the lie worked. Isaac gave Jacob his blessing.

3. **How do you feel about what Rebekah and Jacob did?** This is an opportunity to talk about important family issues like lying, favoritism, and trust.

4. **This family is a mess! Read verses 41-45 again. What happens because of all the sin in this family?** The family suffered. Jacob and Esau's relationship came close to the point of murder, just like Cain and Abel. Their family was broken apart, as Jacob had to run for his life. Isaac and Rebekah's marriage was damaged. All of this sin had great consequences.

5. **Perhaps the biggest sin in this story is the sin of lying. Can you think of a time that you told a lie? What happened? How can we help each other as a family to always tell the truth?**

6. **Every member of this family did things wrong. They all suffered because of what they did. But what was God doing through all of this?** God's plan continued. He chose Jacob to be the next leader of the people of Israel. Jacob did indeed become that leader, despite all these problems. We are not on the throne of the Universe. God is. While our sin grieves God, and it hurts us, He has a plan for our family and for the world.

Prayer

A powerful way to pray as a family is to follow the "ACTS" model. You may choose to pray through one or all of these sections. Invite anyone who wants to pray to do so.

ADORATION

In reading the Bible today, what are some of the things that we learned about God? *We learned that God keeps His plan moving even when we sin and make mistakes.* **We can praise Him for that!**

CONFESSION

We have all lied. We have all played favorites. Use this time to confess your sins. *It is valuable for a parent to lead this time with vulnerable confession.*

THANKSGIVING

How has God been faithful to our family? How has He kept His plan moving through the generations? *Thank Him for these things now.*

SUPPLICATION

The story of Isaac, Rebekah, Jacob, and Esau is filled with family problems. Take time now to lift the struggles in your family to God. Ask Him to help you live more like Christ at home every day.

A parent can conclude the family worship time with a prayer of thanks to God.

Growing Together Throughout the Week

Keep the conversation about God and His Word going throughout the week. Consider talking about some of these questions at meal times, in the car, or before bed. Some brief answers are provided to help you guide the conversation.

1. **What does it mean to "play favorites"? In our Bible reading, Isaac and Rebekah had their favorite sons. Isaac loved Esau more. Rebekah**

loved Jacob more. **Have you ever felt like someone was playing favorites with you? How did it make you feel?**

We all feel like this from time to time. We can feel like this at home or with our friends. If you have a child who is feeling like they are "the favorite," or "not the favorite," it is important to get that out in the open so that the family can talk it through and offer forgiveness to each other.

2. **Have you ever been so mad that you wanted to throw something, hit something, or even hurt someone? Esau got so mad about what happened that he wanted to hurt his brother Jacob, and maybe even to kill him. We all struggle with feelings of anger. When we feel angry it is an important moment of testing. What will we do with our anger?**

God doesn't want us to slam doors, throw things, or most of all hurt other people. Instead, when we are angry, we need to pray and ask God to help us act like Jesus in that moment.

3. **What happens when we lie?**

Here are just a few of the terrible things that begin to happen when we lie:

- We feel guilty.
- People stop trusting us.
- We are tempted to lie more to cover up the first lie.
- God will discipline us to bring us to the point where we are ready to confess and ask for forgiveness.

Family Memory Verse

Work together as a family to memorize this verse this week.

The heart of man plans his way, but the LORD establishes his steps. (Proverbs 16:9)

Catechism Questions

As you go through your week, help each other learn the answers to these important questions. You may choose to include catechism as a part of your family worship time.

27. **Who can change a sinner's heart?** The Holy Spirit alone.

28. **What did God give to Moses to summarize His Law?** Ten commandments.

29. **What is the summary of the ten commandments?** To love God with all my heart, and my neighbor as myself.

Digging Deeper—For Teens

Talk about these questions with your teen.

1. **This is a complicated passage of Scripture. Why did God choose Jacob to be the leader of the family and not Esau? God helps us understand more of His decisions in the New Testament. Read Hebrews 12:14–17. What does this tell us about Esau's heart?**

   In Hebrews, Esau is called "godless." Esau knew that God had called the oldest son of the family to become the family leader. He didn't care about God's will. He was willing to trade his life purpose before God for a bowl of soup. We also see Esau's godlessness in his rage and desire to murder Jacob after he lost the blessing. God knew that Esau's heart was wicked.

2. **The Bible is filled with families filled with problems. Many of the historical accounts God chose to give us in the Bible have to do with siblings. Jacob and Esau were fighting with each other even before they were born! What do you think God desires for how brothers and sisters should live together and relate to each other?**

   The world tells us that the best we can hope for is that siblings "get along." God gives us a dramatically different vision in the Bible. If God has blessed you with siblings, He has created spiritual partners for you. He has given you prayer warriors to do battle with you. He has a mission for you and your siblings to accomplish together for Christ and for His Kingdom. What would it take for you and your brothers/sisters to move from just "getting along" to building powerful Christ-centered friendships for the glory of God?

Preschool Fun

Can you figure out what something is without using your eyes? Get four or five objects which have distinct smells or textures. Put a blindfold on your preschooler (a soft cloth bandana works great for this). See if he or she can guess what the objects are just by touching them, or by smelling them. Then trade places. You get to wear the blindfold, and they get to choose the items. If an older sibling or another adult is around, they can help as needed.

You can use this game to help your child understand how Isaac, because he could not see, had a difficult time knowing whether he was talking with Jacob or Esau.

Genesis 32

Jacob Returns Home and Wrestles with God

Activity

Words in **bold** are what you can say to lead this activity.

> Supplies needed: A spool of string (a couple hundred feet) or a spool of fishing line.

We are going to have a great time of family worship tonight. In order to get started, I would like us to move around so that we are sitting in a circle. It will also help if we are all on the same level (everyone in chairs, or everyone on the floor).

Have you ever seen a cool spider web? We are going to make an "encouragement web." Here is how it works. In my hand I have a spool of string. In just a minute I am going to hold on to the end of the string, and then toss the spool to someone in the circle. Once they catch the spool, there will be a line of string between us. I then have a chance to say something encouraging to that person. It is a

chance for me to say something that I appreciate about them or thank them for something nice they did.

Then the person that I encouraged will hold on to the string and toss the spool to someone else. They will encourage that person, who will then toss the spool to someone else and pretty soon you will see our "encouragement web" start to grow!

So let me get things started...

Here are a few things to watch for:

Allow the game to continue so that people receive more than one encouragement. But pay attention if someone is being left out and make a point to encourage them next chance you get.

Do what you can to focus encouragement on character traits rather than on looks or superficial things. "You have nice hair" is not what we are looking for! Instead seek to encourage character traits or actions such as, "I noticed that you cleared the table after dinner without being asked. I really appreciated that." Or, "You are a really good friend." Or, "I see you spend time reading your Bible. I admire that."

Singing

Consider one or more of the following songs to praise God for His faithfulness. Use the resources in the introduction to find music and lyrics for suggested songs.

Do Not Be Anxious, by Seeds Family Worship

Glory to God Forever

Overwhelmed, by Big Daddy Weave

Learn more about SEEDS Family Worship resources - **www.seedsfamilyworship.net**

Scripture Reading: Genesis 32

Read the above Scripture as a family.

The Child's Story Bible by Catherine Vos is a great resource to super-charge your family Bible reading time. It will help your whole family understand how the events of the Bible fit together.

Talk About It

Discuss the following questions as a family. The brief answers provided may help you guide the conversation as needed.

1. **In our last time of family worship, we read about how Jacob had to run away from his brother Esau. Esau was furious because Jacob had tricked their father Isaac into giving him the family blessing. In the chapter we just read, Jacob was finally returning home. How was Jacob feeling about seeing Esau again?** He was terrified. Jacob did not

know if Esau was still angry with him. He was afraid that Esau still wanted to kill him.

2. **What did Jacob do to show Esau that he was sorry for what he did?** He sent respectful messages to Esau. Jacob presented himself as a "servant," and he hoped that he might find favor in Esau's eyes (Gen. 32:4-5). He also sent his servants ahead with gifts for Esau.

3. **Jacob was terribly afraid. He did what God wants us to do when we are afraid. What was that? (Gen. 32:9)** He was afraid, and so Jacob prayed. Look at how Jacob prayed. He prayed the promises of God. He spoke the words of God back to God. He told God he was afraid. He asked God to save him.

4. **After Jacob sent his family and possessions across the river, he spent the night alone. But he was not alone for long. What happened?** We can't understand everything that happened, but the Bible says that Jacob wrestled the entire night with a "man." It seems that this was no ordinary man, but actually the Lord in the form of a man. Jacob kept struggling until finally the Lord touched his hip and wrenched it. Then Jacob seemed to just hang on for dear life because he could not fight anymore.

5. **After the wrestling match, the Lord gave Jacob a new name. What was it and what does it mean?** The name Jacob means "deceiver." Jacob had lived up to his name had he not? At this moment, God was giving Jacob a new identity. He would no longer be known as "deceiver," but as "Israel," a name which means "He strives with God."

6. This is a beautiful story of God taking a broken relationship between two brothers and bringing them back together again. Jacob returned home. Jacob was sorry for lying. He faced his fears and prayed. He "wrestled" with God. God put Jacob's past behind him and gave him a new name and a new future. What lessons can our family learn about working through the hard times and hurt feelings we face together?

Prayer

For your prayer time today, consider using the "High-Low" prayer approach. You can use the words in bold below to help guide you.

In our prayer time I would like us to do "High-Low." To start with, I would like to see if each person would be willing to share the high, or the best part, of their day (or week).

Encourage as many people as possible to share their high points.

Thank you all for sharing those things. Would someone be willing to pray and thank God and give Him praise for all the blessings that were just shared?

If no one is comfortable praying, you can take the lead and thank God for the "highs" that were shared.

Now, would someone be willing to tell us about a "low" from today or from this week? What was the worst part of your day/week?

It is helpful for you to go first when sharing lows. Listen to each person share their lows with the family.

Thank you all for sharing those things. It is so important for us to open our hearts to each other. Would someone be willing to pray and ask God to help us with all the things we have just heard? God loves us and we can bring everything to Him.

If no one is comfortable praying, you can lead this time of prayer, asking God to help each person in your family as they face difficult situations.

Growing Together Throughout the Week

Keep the conversation about God and His Word going throughout the week. Consider talking about some of these questions at meal times, in the car, or before bed. Some brief answers are provided to help you guide the conversation.

1. **Have you ever heard the phrase "the children of Israel"? According to our Bible reading this week from Genesis 32, where did that phrase come from?**

God gave Jacob a new name—Israel. The phrase, "the children of Israel," is another way of saying "the descendants of Jacob."

2. **When was the last time you felt afraid? What did you do?**
   Use this conversation to encourage your children to open up to you about their fears. It may be helpful to share some of your fears with them, or fears that you had when you were their age. Talk about the example of Jacob, who faced his fears with prayer, and asked God to save him. Consider ending the conversation by putting this principle into practice and praying together.

3. **Jacob's wrestling match with God was an important moment in his life. His faith grew. God blessed him. God rescued him from the anger of Esau. It was so important to him that he named the place where it happened "Peniel," which means, "the face of God." Jacob also made sure to tell the story to his descendants, who decided to make sure they would remember the story by not eating the tendon attached to the hip. How does our family do at remembering the ways God has blessed us? Are we doing anything to make sure that future grandchildren and great-grandchildren will know about how God has worked in our family?**
   Encourage your children to come up with creative ways that God's work in your family can be recorded, remembered, and passed on for generations to come.

Family Memory Verse

Work together as a family to memorize this verse this week.

We will not hide them from their children, but tell to the coming generation the glorious deeds of the LORD, and his might, and other wonders that he has done. (Psalm 78:4)

Catechism Questions

As you go through your week, help each other learn the answers to these important questions. You may choose to include catechism as a part of your family worship time.

30. **What effect did the sin of Adam have on all mankind?** All mankind is born in a state of sin and misery.

31. **Can anyone go to heaven with this sinful nature?** No; our hearts must be changed before we can be fit for heaven.

32. **What is a change of heart called?** Regeneration.

Digging Deeper—For Teens

Talk about these questions with your teen.

1. Terrible things happened between these two brothers, Jacob and Esau. They did things that hurt each other deeply. Genesis 32 is a story of the healing of their relationship. What can you learn from the story of Jacob and Esau that might help you make peace in your relationships with siblings or friends?

2. According to the Scriptures, Jacob physically wrestled with the LORD who appeared to him as a man. We don't "wrestle" with God that way, but that doesn't mean that we don't struggle with our faith and struggle to follow and obey God. In what ways do you feel that you "wrestle," or "struggle," with God?

   Parents, you can take the lead in sharing personally about the "wrestling," or "struggling," you have done in your faith journey. This is also an opportunity to encourage your teen to "doubt his/her doubts," and "believe his/her beliefs." Jacob had to face his fear, take it to God in prayer, and act with courage.

3. When Jacob was wrestling with God, he would not let go. He would not give up. He wanted to know God and have God bless him. Sometimes, when life gets hard, we can feel like giving up. Have you ever felt like that? Are you feeling like that now? What would it mean to follow Jacob's example?

Preschool Fun

Time to wrestle! Find an open space and have fun with a good old-fashioned wrestling match. Be careful your preschooler doesn't hurt you! After you are done wrestling, you can talk about what it would be like to wrestle against God. Then read the story about Jacob from Genesis 32.

SUPER-CHARGE YOUR RELATIONSHIP WITH YOUR TEENAGER

Consider getting one of the best books on raising teenagers and preparing them for a lifetime of following God: *The Age of Opportunity,* by Paul David Tripp.

Genesis 37

God Saves Joseph

Activity

Words in **bold** are what you can say to lead this activity.

Supplies needed: A board, hammer, and nails.

Family worship begins with construction! I am going to need everyone's help here.

Bring out the board, the hammer, and the nails.

In just a minute, I am going to ask each person to hammer one nail into this board. You don't need to hammer it in very far, just so that it sticks in there.

But before we do that, I want to tell you what these things represent. The board represents another person. So the board can be one of your siblings, a friend, or maybe even mom or dad. The hammer represents anger. Raise your hand if you

have ever felt anger at someone? What are some of the things that we do when we are angry?

Listen as different family members share what they do when they are angry. This is a good opportunity for you to tell a true story about a time that you allowed your anger to get the best of you.

One of the things we often do when we are angry is use our words to hurt someone else. We yell. We talk back. We use harsh and disrespectful tones. We might even swear. The nails that we have here represent the angry words that we sometimes use.

Here is where I need your help. Let's all take a turn and hammer a nail into the piece of wood. Help smaller children as needed.

When we use our anger to hurt each other, it is like putting a nail into someone. Our anger doesn't hurt their body, but it does hurt their heart! What can we do if we hurt someone with our words? Is there any way to take it back?

Yes, we can admit what we did, say it was wrong, and ask forgiveness.

Because God has forgiven us, we can forgive each other. We can "take out" the nails--the angry, mean things that we say. In fact, let's all do that now.

Give each person a chance to remove his or her nail from the wood. Help little ones as needed.

Thank God that we can forgive each other! But look at the wood. What do you see? There are still holes there. God can "patch up" those holes over time, but the lesson that I want you to learn tonight, and we will see it in our Bible reading today, is that God wants each of us to do our part to keep anger out of our home.

Singing

Consider one or more of the following songs to praise God for His goodness. Use the resources in the introduction to find music and lyrics for suggested songs.

Mouth, by Seeds Family Worship

10,000 Reasons, by Matt Redman

What a Friend We Have in Jesus (suggested version by Keith and Kristyn Getty)

Scripture Reading: Genesis 37

Read the following Scripture out loud as a family. Does one person usually read the Bible during this time? Consider asking someone else to read today.

Talk About It

Discuss the following questions as a family. The brief answers provided may help you guide the conversation as needed.

1. **The chapter we just read is the start of an incredible true story. We meet this young man Joseph. He is the son of Jacob, the grandson of Isaac, and the great-grandson of Abraham. The story begins with a big problem. What is that problem according to Genesis 37:3?** Israel (remember that this is the new name that God gave to Jacob) loved Joseph more than his other sons. He was his favorite.

2. **Can you think of other times in the book of Genesis that we have seen the sin of favoritism in a family? What happens to families when people play favorites?** Perhaps the most dramatic example is with Jacob and Esau. Esau was his father's favorite and Jacob was his mother's favorite. Favoritism destroys relationships. It hurts everyone in the family very deeply.

3. **Joseph had two dreams. What did he dream and what did he do about it?** He dreamed that his brothers would one day bow at his feet and serve him. It seems that Joseph acted like a brat and bragged about his dreams. Even his father rebuked him.

4. **His brothers were furious with Joseph. What did they plan to do to him?** Their anger had boiled up to the point of violence. They made plans to kill him. This is not the first time in the Bible we have seen

anger between siblings move toward murder: Cain and Abel; Jacob and Esau; Now Joseph and his brothers.

5. **Anger destroys relationships between brothers and sisters, and can even lead to violence. Is there anger in your heart today toward one of your siblings or toward another member of your family? If so, can we ask forgiveness from one another right now so that God can set us free from our anger?**

6. **God moved in the heart of Reuben to try and save Joseph's life. In the end, the brothers sold him into slavery. They went home and lied to their father about what had happened. Would you say that God saved Joseph or God abandoned Joseph? Why?** Joseph's brothers planned on killing Joseph, but God had other plans. God provided a way of escape for him, in spite of his brothers's sins. Joseph did not want to be sold into slavery, but God was leading him to a special mission and purpose.

7. **Can you think of a time that God allowed something hard or painful to happen to you because God was leading you into an important mission or purpose?**

Prayer

For your prayer time today, consider using the "High-Low" prayer approach. You can use the words in bold below to help guide you.

In our prayer time I would like us to do "High-Low." To start, I would like to see if each person would be willing to share a high, or best part, of their day (or week).

Encourage as many people in the family that are willing to share their high points.

Thank you all for sharing those things. Would someone be willing to pray and thank God and give Him praise for all the blessings that were just shared?

If no one is comfortable praying, you can take the lead and thank God for the "highs" that were shared.

Now, would someone be willing to tell us about a "low" from today or from this week? What was the worst part of your day/week?

It is helpful for you to go first when sharing "lows." Listen to each person share their lows with the family.

Thank you all for sharing those things. It is so important for us to open our hearts to each other. Would someone be willing to pray and ask God to help us with all the things we have just heard? God loves us and we can bring everything to Him.

If no one is comfortable praying, you can lead this time of prayer, asking God to help each person in your family as they face difficult situations.

Growing Together Throughout the Week

Keep the conversation about God and His Word going throughout the week.

Consider talking about some of these questions at meal times, in the car, or before bed. Some brief answers are provided to help you guide the conversation.

1. **Have you ever felt hurt because of favoritism? What does it feel like when a teacher, a friend, or even someone in the family treats you as less important than someone else?**
   Parents, this is a good opportunity for you to share about a time that you were hurt by favoritism. It will help your son or daughter open up. You may even ask him or her directly if he or she ever feels that you play favorites in the family. Be prepared for an honest answer, and be ready to apologize for any hurts you may have caused.

2. **Joseph's brothers did a terrible thing when they sold Joseph into slavery. But what did they do next, and what lesson can we learn from it?**
   They pretended that Joseph and been killed and lied to their father Jacob. When we sin, Satan always tempts us to add another sin on top of it. Often times, the second sin is the sin of lying in order to cover up the first wrong thing we did. The lesson is that when we sin, we should tell the truth and repent quickly, not add another sin on top of it.

3. **Can you think of a time that you did one thing wrong, and then lied to cover it up? Did the lie make things better or worse?**
   Parents, take this opportunity to tell your kids about a time that you lied to cover up one of your sins and the added consequences that you faced for taking one sin and turning it into two.

Family Memory Verse

Work together as a family to memorize this verse this week.

As for you, you meant evil against me, but God meant it for good, to bring it about that many people should be kept alive, as they are today. (Genesis 50:20)

Catechism Questions

As you go through your week, help each other learn the answers to these important questions. You may choose to include catechism as a part of your family worship time.

33. **Who will be saved from the penalty of sin?** Only those who repent and place their faith alone in the Lord Jesus Christ.

34. **What does it mean to repent?** To change my mind about sin and God, which leads to a change of my behavior as empowered by the Holy Spirit.

35. **What does it mean to believe or have faith in Christ?** To trust in Christ alone for salvation.

Digging Deeper—For Teens

Consider talking about these questions with your teen

1. **Genesis 37 is filled with the destruction of "generational patterns." Joseph's brothers seek to murder him, just like their uncle Esau wanted to do to their father Jacob. The brothers lie to their father Jacob. Jacob lied to his father Isaac. What does this tell us about the nature of sin?**

   Sin can infect entire families. If left unchecked and un-repented of, sinful patterns can be passed down generationally. When one generation sins, the next generation is often damaged and infected by that sin.

2. **Can you identify any generational patterns in your family, both good and bad?**

   List some positive character traits that have been passed down through the generations of your family. Then discuss or list some sins and negative character traits that are spread through your family. Parents, humbly take the lead in this. Talk openly about sinful patterns in your parents that replicated in your life.

3. **If you identify sinful patterns that keep getting repeated in your family tree, take time together and pray against those sins. Ask God to apply the grace and power of the cross to those generational patterns so that they might be broken and not infect your generation and the future generations of your family.**

Preschool Fun

What do you think Joseph's special coat looked like? Do your best to make a coat-of-many-colors with your preschooler. You might use construction paper, or a collection of brightly colored clothes, bandanas, or sheets. In Joseph's family, his father Jacob played favorites and only gave a special coat to Joseph. Don't make the same mistake. Work with your preschooler to make a special coat for every child in the family. When you give them the coat let them know how much you love them all!

SUPERCHARGE YOUR FAMILY WORSHIP

Doing something new can often feel strange and uncomfortable, but family worship is a great opportunity to learn and grow together.

For example, singing together as a family may be something you don't feel comfortable doing, or something you tend to skip whenever possible. But singing can be a powerful way to engage our hearts in worship of God, and little children love to do it! Be bold and try singing as a family this week!

Or maybe the catechism questions seem overwhelming. Take a chance! See what God will do. You may be surprised how God uses the process of learning those questions to deepen your faith and draw your family closer together.

Genesis 39–50

God Saves Joseph and His Family

Activity

Words in **bold** are what you can say to lead this activity.

Supplies needed: None

Believe it or not we are almost done with our journey through the book of Genesis. We will be starting Exodus soon! For our family worship time tonight, we are going to think back through some of the true stories and lessons that we have learned as we have been reading Genesis.

Here is the plan. I'd like to invite each person to think of a story that we have learned about during family worship in the past few weeks or months. Ideally, it will be something from Genesis. Your job is to act out the story for us, and we have to guess what story you are doing. You can ask other family members to be a part of your story if you need extra people or props. You can dress up or use items from around the house to help tell the story.

However, you can't make any noises. No talking. No grunting. You have to silently act out the story, and the rest of us have to try and guess what it is.

I'll give you some time to think about what you want to do. Remember, you can use other family members, even pets if needed, to help tell the story.

Little ones may need help thinking of what they want to act out. Parents, be sure to participate in this too! The kids will love to see you do this.

Encourage each person to give it a try. Be prepared for the kids to ask for the chance to do another round. If time permits, go for it. After everyone is done, give them encouragement and move into the next part of your family worship time.

You all did great! This is our last big time of family worship in the book of Genesis. Next week we will start a new book, the book of Exodus. Let's worship God together and then open our Bibles to see what God would teach us today.

Singing

Consider one or more of the following songs to praise God for His goodness. Use the resources in the introduction to find music and lyrics for suggested songs.

Do Not Fear, by Seeds Family Worship

Blessed Be Your Name, by Matt Redman

Do it Again, by Elevation Worship

Scripture Reading: Genesis 39:19–41:45

The Bible reading today focuses on one aspect of the Joseph story. Please consider reading the entire story from Genesis 39–50 as you go through this week. Perhaps you could read a chapter or two each morning or each evening. Your family will love it...and God will too!

For this particular time of family worship, invite someone to read the following passage. It is on the long side so invite a few people to read as appropriate.

Talk About It

Discuss the following questions as a family. The brief answers provided may help you guide the conversation.

1. **In our last time together, Joseph was sold by his brothers into slavery. It was not fair or right, but God allowed it to happen. Now Joseph was thrown in prison. Again, it was not fair. If you were Joseph how would you have felt?**

   It is easy to be angry at God when bad things happen to us. There is a difference between hating sin and hating God.

2. **Even though Joseph was in jail, he continued to trust in God. God blessed him in the prison and Joseph was given the responsibility of supervising the other prisoners. Later, two of the kings servants,**

a cupbearer and a baker, were thrown into the prison with Joseph.
What happened?

Each of the men had dreams. They asked Joseph to interpret the
dreams. Joseph told them that he could not do it, but that God could.
God revealed to Joseph that the dreams meant that one man would
return to his position in the palace, and that the other man would die.
Joseph would spend another two years in jail.

3. **While Joseph was still in jail, Pharaoh, King of Egypt, also had a
   dream. His wise men could not interpret the dream for him. But
   the cupbearer remembered Joseph, who had interpreted his dream
   when he was in prison. He told Pharaoh about Joseph, and Pharaoh
   summoned him. What did Joseph say when Pharaoh asked him to
   interpret the dream?**

   In Genesis 41:16 Joseph humbly told Pharaoh that he could not do it,
   but that God could. It was a dangerous thing for Joseph to talk about
   the Hebrew God. Pharaoh himself was considered a god. Joseph was
   bold in talking about God. Are we bold when it comes to talking about
   God with our friends and neighbors? Are we bold in talking about
   God in our own family?

4. **God gave Joseph the interpretation of Pharaoh's dream—that there
   would be seven years of plenty and seven years of famine. What
   did Pharaoh do? Pharaoh put Joseph in charge of Egypt! Joseph was
   second only to Pharaoh himself. The mission was unfolding! God**

gave Joseph the assignment of leading the nation of Egypt in order to save them from the coming famine. God brought Joseph through slavery and prison - because God had an important mission for him. What would it take for our family to trust God more when your family is facing hard times?

5. In the final chapters of Genesis, amazing things happen with Joseph and his family. Would you like to take some extra time as a family during the next few days and read the end of this true story together?

If the family wants to finish reading Genesis together, talk about two or three specific times that you can set aside to read together. These extra times in God's word this week will be powerful!

Prayer

A powerful way to pray as a family is to follow the "ACTS" model. You may choose to pray through one or all of these sections. Invite anyone who wants to pray to do so.

ADORATION

In reading the Bible today, what are some of the things that we learned about God? *God protects us. God never abandons us. Even when we are in terrible situations, if we are faithful to Him, we can trust that He is working a good plan for our lives.*

CONFESSION

Joseph chose to believe God even when terrible things were happening to him. Unfortunately, we often feel angry at God and doubt him. Take time and confess any anger or doubts you may be struggling with.

THANKSGIVING

God had a good plan for Joseph, and when we choose to love and follow God, He accomplishes a good plan in our lives too. Thank God that He is in control of our future.

SUPPLICATION

Use this time to pray for the desires of your heart. Pray for faith. Pray for God to show you His plan for your family. Pray for God to use your family to bless the families around you.

A parent can conclude the family worship time with a prayer of thanks to God.

Growing Together Throughout the Week

Keep the conversation about God and His Word going throughout the week. Consider talking about some of these questions at meal times, in the car, or before bed. Some brief answers are provided to help you guide the conversation.

1. **After God helped Joseph to interpret the dream of the baker, he asked him to put in a good word for him with Pharaoh. Joseph wanted to get out of prison, but the baker forgot to tell Pharaoh. Have you had someone let you down or disappoint you? How did you respond?**
   This is an opportunity to remind your kids that people will disappoint them. People will hurt their feelings. Only God is perfect and perfectly trustworthy.

2. **Pharaoh asked Joseph to do something impossible. No human being can interpret someone's dream. Joseph answered Pharaoh by saying, "I cannot do it, but God...," When you face difficult situations, do you try and face them on your own, or do you have the attitude of Joseph: "I cannot do it, but God can." Read John 15:5 and pray together that God will help you rely on Him in everything.**

3. **Think about Joseph's brothers. Joseph had been gone from the family for 13 years. How do you think they were feeling 13 years later after having sold Joseph into slavery?**
   We don't know for sure because the Bible does not tell us. However, as we discover when we keep reading forward in the story, they never forgot what they did to Joseph, and they continued to feel guilty about it.

Family Memory Verse

Work together as a family to memorize this verse this week. It is the same verse as last week because it is perhaps the most important verse in the Joseph story.

As for you, you meant evil against me, but iGod meant it for good, to bring it about that many people should be kept alive, as they are today. (Genesis 50:20)

Catechism Questions

As you go through your week, help each other learn the answers to these important questions. You may choose to include catechism as a part of your family worship time.

36. **Can you repent and believe in Christ by your own power?** No; I can do nothing good without the help of God's Holy Spirit.

37. **What is justification?** It is when God forgives sinners by grace.

38. **What is sanctification?** It is God making sinners holy in heart and conduct.

Digging Deeper—For Teens

Consider talking about these questions with your teen.

1. **The story of Joseph reminds us of a well-known verse in the New Testament. Read Romans 8:28. Many people remember and quote the first half of the verse, without the second half. Does this verse promise that God will work all things for the good of all people?**

   No. God does not promise to work in all things for the good of all people. God promises to work in all things for the good of those who love Him. Joseph is a perfect example of this. Joseph loved God. He believed in Him. He kept his faith. In response to Joseph's faith, God brought him through his suffering and used him for good.

2. **Have you ever had a friend or sibling going through a hard time and tried to encourage them by saying, "Don't worry. It will all work out. It will be OK"? Sometimes we say that to people to cheer them up. But according to Romans 8:28 should we say that to people if they are not seeking to love and follow God?**

   Telling someone, "Don't worry, it will all work out," if they are not seeking to follow God is not a true thing to say. You are giving them false hope. Instead, encourage them to love God and trust Him. If they do that, then you can stand on the authority of the Bible and tell them that God will not abandon them and will see them through.

3. **The story of Joseph is one of unjust suffering. It was not fair for Joseph to be sold into slavery or go to prison. How can we make sense of that?**

Some of the suffering we experience in our lives comes from the consequences of our own sin. At times we suffer unjustly because we live in a fallen world, and other times we suffer because of the sin of others (as happened to Joseph).

Preschool Fun

Find something that glows in the dark. Let your preschooler use a flashlight to "charge up" the glow in the dark object and then quickly take it into a dark room to see what happens. Then sit in the dark room and watch the glow fade away. Teach your preschooler that in order to shine for God we need to live in the light every day.

That means taking time for prayer, Bible reading, and worshipping God with our family both at church and at home.

VISIONARY FAMILY
M I N I S T R I E S

We reach people through our live conferences, books, video Bible Studies, and free internet resources. Here are just some of the ways we may be able to serve you:

Small Group Bible Studies | *Available either as DVDs or streaming content:*

- ‣ Visionary Parenting
- ‣ Visionary Marriage
- ‣ Never Too Late
- ‣ Generations: Following Jesus as a Family
- ‣ Preparing for a Visionary Marriage

Books | *Available in print or as e-books:*

- ‣ Visionary Parenting
- ‣ Visionary Marriage
- ‣ Never Too Late
- ‣ Limited Church: Uniting Church and Family in the Great Commission

Live Conferences and Seminars

We would be honored to partner with you to strengthen and equip parents, couples, and families in your community. To learn more, visit our website: **http://visionaryfam.com/host-a-conference** or call us at 630-215-9399.

CONTACT US TODAY!

WEB
visionaryfam.com

PHONE
630-215-9399

EMAIL
Rob Rienow | rob@visionaryfam.com
Jonathan Ziman | jonathan@visionaryfam.com
Kate Hoffman | kate@visionaryfam.com

🐦 @visionaryfam
📘 Visionary Family Ministries
📷 @VisionaryFamilyMinistries
📍 @visionaryfam

Made in the USA
Lexington, KY
14 May 2018